4.58

Thomas Traherne

Mystic and Poet

BY

K. W. SALTER

NEW YORK

BARNES & NOBLE, INC.

PUBLISHERS · BOOKSELLERS · SINCE 1873

Published in *The United States*
in 1965
by Barnes & Noble, Inc.
105 *Fifth Avenue New York* 3

359606

Printed in Great Britain by
Butler & Tanner Ltd, Frome and London

Contents

Preface

—in truth the great Elements we know of are no mean Comforters—the open Sky sits upon our senses like a sapphire Crown—the Air is our Robe of State—the Earth is our throne and the Sea a mighty Minstrell playing before it.

> John Keats in a letter to Jane Reynolds,
> Sunday, 14 September 1817.

THIS book is not primarily a work of literary criticism, nor would I claim to have made any significantly new contribution to our knowledge of the beliefs and modes of thought of seventeenth-century England. There is certainly an interest today in mysticism, a scholarly and a popular interest, but my concern lies chiefly in pointing out those qualities in the works of Thomas Traherne which may, in a real sense, be of use to a reader in our present times. That is to say, I wish to emphasize in Traherne the dignity of what Keats called the 'Life of Sensations', to explore the meaning of a word now, in some ways, debased, the word, enjoyment, and to attempt to make clear what may be the consequences of that most difficult of virtues, a genuine humility.

K. W. SALTER

University of Exeter,
June 1964.

Introductory

'WHAT a piece of work is a man! How noble in reason! how infinite in faculty! in form, in moving, how express and admirable! in action, how like an angel! in apprehension, how like a god! the beauty of the world! the paragon of animals.'[1] The Jacobean audience would have responded fully to these lines, not only because of their dramatic relevance to the particular situation of the play but also because they expressed a current attitude. This eulogy of Renaissance man is followed immediately by words charged with the weight of medieval theology: 'And yet, to me, what is this quintessence of dust?' The 'goodly frame' of the earth, the 'majestical roof fretted with golden fire' is at the same time 'a foul and pestilent congregation of vapours'. This Janus-like attitude is to a large degree representative of the first half of the seventeenth century. Glorification of the individual is found side by side with the conception of man and nature as fallen and depraved, to be redeemed only by divine grace. Man is a splendid creature; there is also in him a profound weakness. Faustus, in Marlowe's play, after putting the thought of God out of his mind or attempting to do so in the pursuit of a power which he never measures in the play by any but human standards, cries at last on Christ's blood to save him. Edmund, a characteristic Renaissance 'new man', ridicules Gloucester's forebodings[2] which, for all the superstition in them, carry the authority of the medieval conception of an order superior to that 'Wisdom of nature' which attempts to explain events in exclusively rational terms. To Edmund man is what he is, his God is his own nature; let him serve that: 'I should have been that I am, had the maidenliest star in the firmament twinkled on my bastardizing.' Edmund's standards are those of success, and secular success alone; yet in the end he fails even by his own standards. He is false to his own god in attempting to countermand his orders for the execution of Cordelia and Lear: 'Some good I mean to do, Despite of my own nature.'[3] His own supposed control over the course of events is seen to be an illusion. It is in the same play also that man as man alone (without God, that is) is starkly described in Lear's words on seeing Edgar: 'Thou art the thing itself:

---

[1] *Hamlet*, Act II, Sc. ii, 310.
[2] *King Lear*, Act I, Sc. ii, 121.   [3] *King Lear*, Act V, Sc. iii, 242.

I

unaccommodated man is no more but such a poor bare forked animal as thou art.'

It would be improper to offer isolated extracts from the drama as conclusive evidence in support of a view of life existing outside the world of the play itself. We can, however, see them as offering instances of ways of thought and feeling which were active at the time. There is indeed a good deal of evidence in the literature of the early part of the seventeenth century to show the continuing power of traditional beliefs that man needs God and that his life is meaningless unless seen against a background of eternity and orientated to a transcendent end. Sir Thomas Browne (1605–82) saw the world not as 'an Inn but an Hospital; and a place not to live, but to dye in',[1] and Sir William Temple (1628–90) at the end of his *Essay on Poetry* wrote of human life as 'at the greatest and the best, but like a froward child, that must be play'd with and humoured a little to keep it quiet till it falls asleep, and then the case is over'. This world, says Browne, is dependent on another world; it has no real substance in itself: 'Life itself is but the shadow of death, and souls departed but the shadows of the living: All things fall under this name. The sunne itself is but the dark *simulachrum*, and light but the shadow of God.'[2]

Lastly, man needs the continual support of a supernatural power to maintain him as a human being. Without the idea of God towards which he can aspire, and without the active intervention of divine power, he would relapse into the beast:

> If that the heavens do not their visible spirits
> Send quickly down to tame these vile offences,
> It will come,
> Humanity must perforce prey on itself,
> Like monsters of the deep.[3]

Conversely, if man is a noble and splendid creature, it is because he contains within himself that which is more than human. He is to be valued not for himself but because of the god within him: 'There is surely a piece of divinity in us, something that was before the elements, and owes no homage unto the sun.'[4] This view of man involves a

---

[1] Sir Thomas Browne, *Works*, ed. Sayle, 3 vols. (Edinburgh, 1927), vol. I, *Religio Medici*, part II, sect. 11, p. 104.

[2] Sir Thomas Browne, *Works*, ed. cit., vol. III, p. 200.

[3] *King Lear*, Act IV, Sc. ii, 46. (Albany's words here are the same in substance as the opening speech of God in the morality *Everyman*.)

[4] Sir Thomas Browne, *Works*, ed. cit., vol. I, p. 105.

sense of mystery, a conviction that there are, immediately present and active in human society, other than human forces which are not reducible to reason. Yet co-existent with this traditional view of man and his life, there were forces at work in this century in a different direction. These forces were to lead to a separation in men's minds between man and God. The direction of change during this period was towards the isolation of a particular human activity, the power of ratiocination working in conjunction with experimental method and the observation of facts, and its elevation to an all important position. As the authority of reason increased so the conception of God as a being to be apprehended directly, a mysterious yet concrete reality began to recede. The change that was in progress, or rather that aspect of it that I am concerned to remark here in relation to a consideration of the work of Thomas Traherne, is that from the perception of divinity within man, a divinity he possesses by virtue of his participation in a divine order, to the deification of a particular element in human behaviour. Traherne writes always with great confidence in reason since to him it is the image of God within us. By reason, therefore, we may 'discover all the mysteries of heaven'.[1]

Francis Bacon (1561–1626), Thomas Hobbes (1588–1679) and John Locke (1632–1704) all contribute to and are influenced by the forces of change in this century. It is not my purpose to inquire in detail into the thought of these men. I am concerned only with indicating some of the salient features of the world in which Traherne lived. We have seen something already of the continued existence in the seventeenth century of the medieval theological view of man; a further illustration would be provided by Ulysses' great speech in *Troilus and Cressida*: 'The speciality of rule hath been neglected',[2] which takes the form of an argument for order as if this order needed insisting on in a world that was turning from it. It is relevant now to point briefly to some of the evidence which indicates the directions of change. Francis Bacon rejected the Peripatetic-scholastic tradition and proposed a 'transference of interest from abstract speculation to observation of nature'.[3] He was seriously concerned with the study of nature as a means of providing a way to the knowledge of reality unaided by the support of theological dogma. The study of things will reveal the truth. 'There was never a

---

[1] Thomas Traherne, *Centuries of Meditation*, Dobell's Ed. (London, 1908), IV, 81.

[2] *Troilus and Cressida*, Act I, Sc. iii, 78–135.

[3] B. Willey, *The 17th Century Background* (London, 1934), p. 24.

miracle wrought by God to convert an atheist, because the light of nature might have led him to confess a God.'[1] The study of nature without asking the metaphysical questions 'What is the meaning of this event'? or 'For what purposes does this exist?' leads to a study of the relation between observed events, to the answer to the limited question 'What has caused an observed situation to have arisen out of a preceding situation?' The study of the relations between events which are to be considered without any preconceptions of the position they may occupy in a transcendental order of values; this is in fact what Bacon is advocating when he speaks of the necessity 'continually to dwell among things —to establish for ever a true and legitimate union between the experimental and rational faculty'.[2] This is the method of study which is the basic instrument of modern science. What is to be noted here is that Bacon was concerned with excluding the metaphysical questions and with concentrating on those questions dealing with physical objects in themselves. He implies, that is, that there are various provinces of study and that it is necessary to isolate one province from another: 'There is truth of religion, and truth of science; and these different kinds of truth must be kept separate.'[3]

In *De Augmentis* Bacon writes: 'We are obliged to believe the word of God, though our reason be shocked at it. For if we should believe only such things as are agreeable to our reason, we assent to the matter and not to the author.'[4] The significant point in this passage is the implied difference between the world of 'the matter' and that of the 'author'. Certainly in this passage there is also the idea that both sides of the division have just claims and this is clearly and without irony stated in the words from the *Novum Organum*: 'It is therefore most wise soberly to render unto faith the things that are faith's.'[5] What I am content to remark here is that a separation is made and, especially, that the standards applicable to the one world are not applicable to the other.[6] Reason can be satisfied in its own field, in the other it may be shocked. Conversely the broad assumption of the words from the *Novum Organum* is that there are subjects with which faith is not con-

---

[1] Bacon, *Advancement of Learning* (ed. 1608), Book II, iv.
[2] Bacon, Preface to *De Augmentis* (Bohn Ed.), p. 16.
[3] B. Willey, *The 17th Century Background*, p. 27.
[4] Bacon, *De Augmentis* (Bohn Ed.), Book IX, p. 368.
[5] Bacon, *Nov. Org.*, ed. Fowler (Oxford, 1889), I, LXV, p. 248.
[6] 'Many things are true in Divinity, which are neither inducible by reason, nor confirmable by sense.' Browne, *Works*, ed. cit., vol. I, *Religio Medici*, p. 67.

cerned. The division is between the world of nature and the word of God, of divine revelation: 'The knowledge of man is as the waters, some descending from above, and some springing from beneath; the one informed by the light of nature, the other inspired by divine revelation.'[1] Both sources will reveal God's purpose; but, and this is the relevant point, both may do so independently of each other. This is the direction in which change was taking place. If nature will reveal reality and if the findings of experiment are verifiable by the 'rational faculty', what place then has the study of God in man's life? If nature can lead to God, why not throw all one's effort on the study of nature while only preserving the idea of a deity as the necessary *primum mobile*?

The distinction between the light of nature on the one hand, and divine revelation on the other, is found also in the work of Sir Thomas Browne: 'There are two Books from whence I collect my Divinity, besides that written, one of God, another of His servant Nature, that Universal and publick Manuscript, that lies expans'd unto the Eyes of all; those that never saw Him in the one, have discovered Him in the other.'[2] In Browne, generally speaking, a balance is maintained between the two scriptures, one to be read by faith, the other by reason. He moves easily from one to the other. The direction of change however was towards an upsetting of this balance. The two scriptures began to show different readings and the one began to be preferred to the other. Thomas Hobbes published his *Leviathan* in 1651, and *De Corpore* in 1655, provoking a 'storm in England comparable only to the ferment excited by the theories of Darwin in the 19th century'.[3] Hobbes had nothing but contempt for the residual effects of the old theological view of man and his life. The supernatural mystery of religion is fit only for the '*Kingdom of fairies* ,and the 'old wives *fables* in England concerning *ghosts* and *spirits*, and the feats they play in the night'.[4] The religious experience of the presence of God as a force penetrating the material world is dismissed with the remark: 'What kind of felicity God hath ordained to them that devoutly honour Him, a man shall no sooner know, than enjoy; being joys, that now are so incomprehensible, as the word of Schoolmen *beatifical vision* is unintelligible.'[5] Intelligibility

---

[1] Bacon, *Advancement of Learning* (ed. 1605), book II, v. i.
[2] Browne, *Works*, ed. cit., vol I, *Religio Medici*, p. 25.
[3] M. Carré, *Phases of Thought in England* (Oxford, 1949), p. 259.
[4] Hobbes, *Leviathan*, ed. Oakeshott (Oxford, 1946), p. 457.
[5] *Ibid.*, p. 39.

was for Hobbes the great test, and the most intelligible method of inquiry was that of the mathematician: 'And, therefore, they that study natural philosophy study in vain, except they begin at geometry; and such writers or disputers thereof, as are ignorant of geometry, do make their readers and hearers lose their time.'[1]

Still later in the century we find John Locke (1632–1704) writing these words: 'Whatever God hath revealed is certainly true; no doubt can be made of it. This is the proper object of faith; but whether it be a *divine* revelation or no, reason must judge,'[2] and he is so convinced that 'Reason must be our last judge and guide in everything'[3] that he writes sometimes 'as if revelation were by comparison, untrustworthy or superfluous'.[4] The frontiers of natural causation were being pushed back and the road cleared for the deism of the eighteenth century.

It is against this background of ideas and beliefs that the work of Thomas Traherne must be considered. He was a man of intellectual ability though not primarily a philosopher; he had certain gifts of poetic expression but, above all, he achieved a power of mystical vision and was moved to write down the fruits of his experience of this vision in the most remarkable and compelling prose. The mystical vision he enjoyed, and his reflections on it maintain him, in the changing world of his time, to a position of stable equilibrium. He saw man, God and nature as essentially related. The study of nature cannot be separated from the study of God:

> Natural Philosophy—taking it as it is usually bounded in its terms, it treateth only of corporeal things, as Heaven, Earth, Air, Water, Fire, the Sun and Stars, Trees, Herbs, Flowers—with all other beings of that kind. And as thus it is taken it is nobly subservient to the highest ends: for it openeth the riches of God's Kingdom and the natures of his territories . . . (*Centuries of Meditation*, III, 44).

The phrase 'nobly subservient to the highest ends' is the key to the position of Traherne. I call it a balance; it is so because of his vision of the universe as an order in which all things when rightly understood are in balanced harmony. Thus Traherne writes of nature in almost

---

[1] Elements of Philosophy (the trans. of *De Corpore*), *The English Works of Thomas Hobbes*, ed. W. Molesworth (London, 1839–45), vol. I, p. 73.

[2] John Locke, *Essay on Human Understanding*, ed. Fraser, 2 vols. (Oxford, 1894), vol. II, p. 425.

[3] Ibid., p. 438.

[4] B. Willey, *The 17th Century Background*, p. 282.

Baconian terms: 'It is impossible for language, miracles or apparitions to teach us the infallibility of God's word, or to show us the certainty of true religion, without a clear sight into truth itself, that is into the truth of things.' This devotion to the 'truth of things' is in the great seventeenth-century tradition; but for Traherne it is not mathematical or geometrical truth, however, which provides certainty. He continues: 'which will themselves when truly seen, by the very beauty and glory of them, best discover and prove religion' (*Centuries*, III, 45). 'When truly seen' implies that, normally, they are not so seen, and, as will appear, it is not reason alone that enables the observer to see truly; he must have cleansed his own sight first, and undergone the transformation of being which is necessary to achieve the purity of the childlike vision. These words of Traherne may seem to give support to the new scientific attitude; they do so; they are expressive also of the desire of the mystic to see God and for first-hand experience of divine order in the world of things. Instead of the dualism which was developing between faith and reason, between the world of science and that of religion, we find in Traherne a vision of human life as part of a larger unity, a unity of an infinite diversity of parts, each part connecting and connected with the other. The life of reason is part of the life of the complete human being and the life of this being is not isolated from nature or from God; it forms part of an order to which it contributes and from which it receives its value. Splendid as he may be, man does not provide a sufficient justification for himself in himself alone.[1] The value of human life and what, today, we would call human values are based on the existence within the human being of that which is more than human. The purpose of life, as Traherne sees it, is to realize that element in our being, 'so piecing this life with the life of Heaven, and seeing it as one with all Eternity, a part of it, a life within it' (*Centuries*, IV, 93).

The importance of Traherne in his own day constitutes also the relevant reason why he should be studied today. He maintains a view of an ordered and unified existence; the various activities of human beings, the different aspects of being which are studied and measured ought not to be regarded as separate ends in themselves, he insists. They should all be directed to the proper end of human life and this end is not simply the discovery of reality; it is the enjoyment of reality, an enjoyment which is 'immediately near to the very gates of our senses' (*Centuries*, I, 23). This is the supreme happiness possible to men. It is a

---

[1] 'That anything may be found to be an infinite treasure its place must be found in Eternity and in God's esteem' (*Centuries*, III, 55).

mystery, beyond rational analysis, 'the mystery of Felicity' (*Centuries*, II, 100).

The great scholar Meric Casaubon viewing with dismay the spread of Hobbes' geometrical method into the field of politics and morals wrote in a letter to Peter du Moulin (Cambridge 1669): 'Men that are much fixed upon matter and secondary causes and sensual objects, if great care be not taken, may in time (there be many examples) and by degrees forget that there be such things in the world of spirits . . . and at last that there is a God and that their souls are immortal.' The counter-balance to the forgetfulness shadowed in these words lies in Traherne's prose: 'Above all trades, above all occupations this is most sublime. This is the greatest of affairs. Whatever else we do it is only in order to this end that we may live conveniently and to enjoy the world and God within it; which is the sovereign employment including and crowning all; the celestial life of a glorious creature, without which all other estates are servile and impertinent' (*Centuries*, IV, 50).

CHAPTER I

The Life of Traherne

THE actual date of Traherne's birth is still uncertain, but the Record of Admissions at Oxford gives the information that on 1 March 1652, on his entry into Brasenose College, Traherne was fifteen years old. The calendar year at that period began on 25 March, so by modern reckoning this date would be 1 March 1653. He must have reached the canonical age of 23 for deacon's orders when he was episcopally ordained, which was on 20 October 1660. This points to 1637 as the year of his birth, and on a date not far from this.

Anthony à Wood gives a brief biographical note in *Athenae Oxonienses*. In the first edition[1] he states that Traherne was 'a Herefordshire man born', and the later edition[2] reads 'A shoe-maker's son of Hereford'. Aubrey confirms this in his *Miscellanies*. Traherne himself makes no mention of his father's occupation but there are frequent allusions to the poverty of the family. He speaks of himself as one 'who in this life am born to mean things according to the world', 'sitting in a little obscure room in my father's house' (*Centuries*, III, 16). There is a possibility, however, according to Gladys Wade[3] that Thomas and his brother Philip may have gone at an early age to a well-to-do relative, Philip Traherne, an inn-keeper and twice mayor of Hereford, If this were so it might explain that before he went to Oxford Traherne seems to have received his education privately. His name, and that of his brother Philip, do not appear on the rolls of the grammar school attached to the cathedral at Hereford, a school which had the right to present certain selected boys to scholarships at Brasenose; and Traherne entered Brasenose as a commoner and paid the usual fees.

On 1 March 1653 Traherne was 'entered a Commoner of Brasenose College'. Anthony à Wood records this and the College Registers confirm it. He was matriculated on the following 2 April. Oxford had, by the time of Traherne's entrance, recovered from the disorganization

---

[1] Vol. II (1692), p. 388.
[2] Ed. Bliss (1813–20), vol. III, p. 1016.
[3] Gladys I. Wade, *Thomas Traherne* (Princeton, 1946).

of its life occasioned by the presence of the King's Headquarters and its transformation into a garrison town during the Civil War. It was settling down, too, from the effects of the 'reforms' instituted by the victorious Parliament and enforced by their appointed Visitors. In particular, Brasenose was peacefully composed by 1653 under the strict governance of its Puritan principal, Dr Greenwood. It was a sober-minded and serious Oxford in which Traherne's undergraduate days were passed and in one of the most Puritan of colleges. In Brasenose, it is recorded, 'every Tutor . . . at some convenient time between the houres of seven and tenne in the evening "was to" cause their Pupills to repair to their chambers to pray with them'.[1] These were the directions of the Parliamentary Visitors, and Greenwood had been appointed by them; no doubt they were faithfully carried out together with the further injunction that all bachelors of arts and undergraduates should 'every Lord's Day' give 'an account . . . of the sermons they have heard and their attendance on other religious exercises on that day'.[2] It is interesting to remark that Joseph Glanvill (1636–80) was a contemporary of Traherne at Oxford. Glanvill entered Exeter College in 1652 and, as Anthony à Wood relates, regretted not having gone to Cambridge. Glanvill was an admirer of the Cambridge Platonists, especially of Henry More, and, it would seem, the 'new Philosophy' was not so highly thought of at Oxford as at Cambridge. Certainly one finds in the work of Traherne evidence of the more traditional, and more disparaged, influence of Aristotle and Aquinas (for instance *Centuries*, III, 64) as well as that of the more 'modern' Plato. Quite possibly, this was an Oxford influence.

We know nothing of the events of his life in Oxford from the time of his admission to the taking of his first degree of Bachelor of Arts on 13 October 1656. He wrote in after years, however, certain comments on Oxford which are illuminating. He is writing from the point of view of one who has realized the order and stability which is one of the fruits of the mystical experience:

Having been at the University, and received there the taste and tincture of another education, I saw that there were things in this world of which I never dreamed; glorious secrets, and glorious persons past imagination. There I saw that Logic, Ethics, Physics, Metaphysics, Geometry, Astronomy, Poesy, Medicine, Grammar, Music, Rhetoric, all kinds of Arts, Trades and Mechanisms that adorned the world pertained to Felicity: at least there I saw those

---

[1] *Visitors Register*, July 1653.   [2] *Visitors Register*, June 1653.

things, which afterwards I knew to pertain unto it: and was delighted in it. There I saw into the nature of the Sea, the Heavens, the Sun, the Moon and Stars, the Elements, Minerals and Vegetables, all which appeared like the King's Daughter all glorious within (*Centuries*, III, 36).

'Taste and tincture'—the words express Traherne's attitude towards learning; that which is to be incorporated into his whole being with the vividness of sensory experience, to be delighted in 'like the King's Daughter'. There are other passages, too, which refer to his years at Oxford and which criticize the University curricula. There was no co-ordinating principle underlying the various subjects of study. Again Traherne is writing in after years and in the light of his subsequent experience. Having realized a unifying principle in his life he was keenly aware, in retrospect, of its absence at Oxford:

> Nevertheless some things were defective too. There was never a tutor that did professly teach Felicity, though that be the mistress of all other sciences. Nor did any of us study these things but as *Aliena*, which we ought to have studied as our own enjoyments. We studied to inform our knowledge, but knew not for what end we studied. And for lack of aiming at a certain end we erred in the manner (*Centuries*, III, 37).

The last sentence contains an idea which is fundamental in Traherne's thought. Means and ends cannot be separated. No one of the objects of human thought and contemplation should be isolated from the other; they must all be 'nobly subservient to the highest ends' and the highest end is the pursuit of Felicity, which was the term Traherne used for the enjoyment of the beatific vision which in these very same years Hobbes was ridiculing as 'unintelligible'. Traherne pays, though, a profound tribute to the University: 'Howbeit there we received all those seeds of knowledge that were afterwards improved; and our souls were awakened to a discerning of their faculties, and exercise of their powers' (*Centuries*, III, 37).

After he took his first degree, Traherne, again to quote Anthony à Wood, 'left the House for a time, and entered into the sacred function'. Over a year passed between October 1656 when he took this degree and December 1657 when he was appointed to the living of Credinhill in the county of Hereford. Probably he returned to Hereford for a while. In two places he refers to a time of comparative leisure in the country: 'When I came unto the country, and being seated among silent trees, and meads and hills, had all my time in mine own hands ...' (*Centuries*, III, 46) and 'When I came unto the country and saw that

I had all the time in my hands . . .' (*Centuries* III, 52). Both passages are of importance in tracing the spiritual progress of Traherne and will be discussed later in that connection. At the moment I am concerned with events in his physical life. Fourteen months later he was appointed to the living of the parish of Credinhill; a record of this appointment is contained in the Lambeth Palace Library:

> Thomas Traherne, cl Admitted the 30th Day of December 1657 to the R. of Crednell als. Creddenhill in the County of Hereford Upon a pres: . . . from Amabella Countesse Dowager of Kent, the Patronesse thereof, And certificates from Wm. Voyle, Wm. Lowe, Samuel Smith, George Primrose, Robert Breton, Benjamin Baxter of Upton upon Seaverne, John Chomley.[1]

The men who sponsored Traherne were all known and convinced Puritans: Voyle, Lowe, and Primrose were 'the leading Puritan clergy of Hereford city',[2] appointed by Parliament after the extrusion of the clergy of the Established Church. Traherne does not appear to be concerned with the controversies of the politics of religion to judge from the *Centuries* or from *Christian Ethics*, though one must point to the notable exception of *Roman Forgeries* which was published later in his life, in 1673. However, it is clear that he must have been well thought of by the Puritan authorities.

He does not seem to have entered at once on his duties as rector of Credinhill; he was in his twentieth year in 1657 and the minimum age to be attained before he could legally take up his office as rector was twenty-three. There is record amongst the Oxford Diocesan Registers of Traherne's ordination by Bishop Skinner of Oxford on 20 October 1660. His suitability as a candidate for presentation to a benefice would presumably have been scrutinized by the commission set up in accordance with the ordinance of 20 March 1654.[3] This was the first of a series of enactments to establish administrative machinery for the selection of the ministry for the State Church. The commission was empowered to pass judgement rather upon the 'fitness of a candidate for service in the Establishment than upon his qualifications for ordination'.[4] Each candidate was required to provide testimonials from at least three persons 'of known godliness and integrity', of whom one must be a minister who could vouch from personal knowledge of the 'holy and

[1] Lambeth Palace Library MS. 999, f. 161.

[2] Gladys Wade, op. cit., p. 62.

[3] *Mercurius Politicus*, 21 March, 23 March, 1654.

[4] W. Jordan, *The Development of Religious Toleration in England 1640–1660* (London, 1938), p. 157.

good conversation' of the candidate.[1] The rights of patrons were maintained except that a patron was not permitted to present a benefice to a person regarded as unsuitable by the commission.

Richard Baxter, who was no fanatic but a courageous critic both of the Protectorate and of ecclesiastical policy in the years following the Restoration, wrote of this commission, which was mainly Independent and Presbyterian in its composition, that

> though some few (were) over-busie and over-rigid . . . against all that were Arminians, and too particular in enquiring after evidence of sanctification in those whom they examined, and somewhat too lax in their admission of unlearned and erroneous men, that favoured Antinomianism and Anabaptism; yet to give them their due, they did abundance of good to the Church . . . so that though there were many of them somewhat partial . . . yet so great was the benefit above the hurt, which they brought to the Church, that many thousands of souls blest God for the faithful ministers whom they let in, and grieved when the prelatists afterward cast them out.[2]

Traherne's sponsors, at least Voyle, Primrose, Smith and Lowe, were in fact 'cast out' at the Restoration. Traherne was confirmed in his benefice, which he does not seem to have visited until 1661. Probably he spent some of the period between 1657 and the taking up of his duties at Credinhill at Oxford. He was ordained as deacon and priest at Launton in October 1660[3] and received the degree of Master of Arts in 1661.

In the absence of more evidence it does not seem possible to arrive at any positive conclusion on a point which may well call for comment, that here we see a man who was vouched for by Puritan clergy before the Restoration and ordained by an Anglican bishop afterwards. It should be pointed out, however, that the date of his ordination is also that of his attainment of the age, twenty-three, when he could lawfully take up his office as rector. Furthermore it appears that the commission, the triers, allowed a wide degree of tolerance in their examinations in the case of intending clergy outside London. Many 'sound Anglican clergyman had taken the Covenant and had satisfied the triers without substantial difficulties of conscience'.[4] Bishop Skinner, who ordained Traherne, and Bishop King continued to ordain a new succession of

[1] Scobell, *Acts and Ordinances* (1658), II, p. 280.

[2] Baxter, *Reliquiae Baxterianae* (1696), I, p. 72.

[3] MS. Oxford diocesan papers d. 106, folio 3. (The Oxford diocesan records are deposited in the Bodleian.)

[4] Jordan, op. cit., p. 200.

clergy throughout the period of the Commonwealth and Protectorate.[1] The interval between presentation and ordination does not necessarily imply that Traherne was being accommodating over matters of high principle. However, any supposition should be avoided in view of the slender evidence.

Our knowledge of the details of Traherne's life at Credinhill is as imperfect as that of the other periods of his life. The village itself lies four miles to the north-east of Hereford and here Traherne found himself with the spiritual care of the small community in his charge. This could have been an occasion to communicate and practise the Christianity he professed: 'For besides contemplative, there is an active happiness, which consisteth in blessed operations. And as some things fit a man for contemplation, so there are others fitting him for action. Which as they are infinitely necessary to practical happiness, so are they likewise infinitely conducive to contemplative itself' (*Centuries*, IV, 1). Traherne writes also that one should think of oneself as a physician, with the duty of healing those who were diseased. 'I need therefore the oil of pity and the balm of love to remedy and heal them' (*Centuries*, IV, 20). The priest must cure evil; sin is an illness which can be remedied. Sin is a lack of order, a disruption of a state of harmony, and the priest must 'like a God, bring Light out of Darkness, and order out of confusion' (*Centuries*, IV, 21). Traherne envisages the relation between the priest and his parishioners, and, on a larger scale, between the seeker for felicity and the world of men and things in which he must live, as essentially reciprocal. The bringing of order into the lives of those who are in disorder does not only benefit the sufferers; it is itself a means to Felicity for the healer; 'To think the world therefore a general Bedlam, or place of madmen, and oneself a physician, is the most necessary point of present wisdom: an important imagination, and the way to Happiness' (*Centuries*, IV, 20), and he writes further that the 'very miseries and sins and offences' that are in the world 'are the materials of his joy and triumph and glory' (*Centuries*, IV, 21). Perhaps we can think of his parishioners at Credinhill as those

> Towards whom, before whom, among whom he might do the work of fidelity and wisdom, exercise his courage and prudence, show his temperance and bring forth the fruits of faith and repentance. For all those are the objects of our joy that are the objects of our care. They are our true treasures about whom we are wisely employed (*Centuries*, IV, 19).

---

[1] E. H. Plumptre, *Life of Thomas Ken* (London, 1890), vol. I, p. 54.

Traherne sees the men and women with whom he deals as instrumental in the achievement of his own sense of order and harmony; but he does not merely use them for his own spiritual purposes. What he is saying is that if one lives wholeheartedly in and for some other object, then one is, in effect, providing oneself with the most profound satisfaction;[1] and this satisfaction will come not as that which is directly aimed at, but as a by-product of this other activity. This is on the level of ethics; but Traherne conceives the joy which results from complete devotion to an object considered as existing outside the self, as having a higher sanction. It is the realization of Christ within the self. Religion transcends ethics, that is, but it cannot dispense with ethics. Traherne's position is summed up in these words: 'He conceived it his duty and much delighted in the obligation, that he was to treat every man in the whole world as representative of mankind, and that he was to meet him, and to pay unto him all the love of God, Angels and Men' (*Centuries*, IV, 27), and finally: 'He thought that he was to treat every man in the person of Christ. That is both as if himself were Christ in the greatness of his love, and also as if the man were Christ . . .' (*Centuries*, IV, 28).

The balanced poise of duty and delight is a parallel to the conception that the 'objects of our care' are the 'objects of our joy' precisely because they are objects of care. It is another expression of the essentially reciprocal relation between the individual self and its environment which Traherne achieves and which, he claims, is possible to others if they will put themselves, in his phrase, 'in frame'. This for Traherne is to 'have a mind composed of Divine Thoughts, . . . to be like Him within' (*Centuries*, I, 10). It is when this state of being has been reached that duty becomes delight, that the parishioners of Credinhill could become not only the objects of his care but also the objects of his joy:[2] 'Seeing the value of their souls through their bodies and prising all things clearly with a due esteem', their rector, in return, 'is arrived here to the estate of immortality' (*Centuries*, IV, 29).

However, the years of Traherne's active ministry at Credinhill were brief enough; he may have left the village in 1667 or, as Margoliouth thinks, in 1669. It was a period, probably, of importance in the development of his religious life. I propose however to consider his spiritual progress in a succeeding chapter and I shall confine myself therefore to

---

[1] Cf. Love 'doth good to its own soul while it doth good to another' (*Centuries*, IV, 59).

[2] 'Then are we blessed when we are a blessing' (*Centuries*, IV, 47).

the further events of his outward life in so far indeed as this implied distinction is valid. There remain two points to remark of his residence at Credinhill. First, it is likely that it became his custom to write down his reflections on his religious experiences during this time. In the Preface to the *Contemplation*[1] (there are two prefaces, and the second, from which I quote, contains a brief biographical note) we read that it was his practice 'most of his time at home' to 'digest his notions of these things into writing'. Miss Wade is of the opinion[2] that this work was written before he went to Teddington and London, that is, before 1669. I find no reason to disagree with her. If this is so then what we know as the *Centuries of Meditation*, his finest work, may have been begun at Credinhill. Second, at some time during this period or perhaps during Traherne's second residence at Oxford he made the acquaintance of Mrs Susanna Hopton. This lady is important because, if for no other reason, it was through her that at least three of Traherne's manuscripts survived. It is very likely too that the Centuries were written for her spiritual guidance.[3]

Before her marriage Mrs Hopton had reacted to the success of the Puritan party by becoming a Catholic. However, at the Restoration and shortly after her marriage with Richard Hopton she returned to the Church of England. Hopton had received considerable lands and leases in Herefordshire as a reward for his services to the crown, and was a chief justice on the Welsh circuit. They lived chiefly at Kington, which is fifteen miles from Credinhill, and the house became the centre of a religious group, 'a family', similar to the better-known community of Little Gidding of which Nicholas Ferrar was the leading spirit. It is very probable that Traherne himself was a member of this Hereford-shire group which lived a life of rule, following the spirit of the discipline of the cloister while living in the world. In the preface to *A Collection of Meditations and Devotions in Three Parts* (published by Nathaniel Spinckes in 1717) there is an account of her way of life:

> She was well known to keep up a constant Course of Devotion, not only in herself, but in her Family, and not only on the Lord's Day, but through-out the whole week, setting apart five times every day for religious worship; from which she would not suffer herself to be diverted by any business that

---

[1] *A Serious and Patheticall Contemplation of the Mercies of God in several most Devout and Sublime Thanksgivings for the same* (1699).

[2] Op. cit., p. 146.

[3] See Wade, op. cit., p. 79.

was not very extraordinary. Even in her Old Age, and the cold winter Season, she would be up, and in the Closet at her Mattins, by four of the Clock in the Morning. From which Customs she was for a long time not to be discouraged, either by the Effects of her declining Age or by the Extremity of Weather. . . . She neither indulged herself in Diet nor sleep, but contented herself with less in both respects than those about her judged convenient for her, so much was she above gratifying the Flesh. . . . She was a constant Observer of not only the Feasts, but Fasts, of the Church, and was much scandalised at the generality of those who profess themselves Members of the Church of England for showing no more regard to such Days. . . .

When he left Credinhill Traherne left certain of his manuscripts with Mrs Hopton, who had one of these printed in 1699; it is the *Contemplation*. It was in the second preface to this work that Bertram Dobell in the first years of the twentieth century found an important clue to the identity of the author of the unidentified manuscript in his possession.[1] Dobell was convinced that the author of his manuscript was the same man who had written the *Contemplation*; and in the preface it is stated that the author had been in 'the service of the late Lord Keeper Bridgeman as his Chaplain'. At the death of Mrs Hopton in 1709, thirty-five years after Traherne's death, more of his manuscripts which had been in her possession passed into the hands of Dr Hickes, a friend. He decided to publish them under the impression that Mrs Hopton was herself the author. He died, however, and his plan was carried out by a common friend, Nathaniel Spinckes. These manuscripts were published in 1717 by Spinckes as the *Hexameron or Meditations on the Six Days of Creation* and *Meditations and Devotions of the Life of Christ*.

In 1669, Traherne took up the duties of private Chaplain to the Lord Keeper of the Seal, Sir Orlando Bridgeman. The Hoptons were influential, Mrs Hopton's family, the Harveys, in particular. One of them was the wife of a solicitor-general during the reign of Charles II, Sir Heneage Finch. Sir Orlando Bridgeman was a distinguished lawyer also, and, according to Miss Wade, a personal friend of Finch.[2] One should not lightly assume, however, that it was the influence of powerful patrons only which secured this post for Traherne. By all accounts[3] Sir Heneage was very careful in scrutinizing the qualifications of

[1] See Appendix I for an account of the discovery of the *Poems* and *Centuries* and the identification of Traherne as their author.

[2] Wade, op. cit., p. 87.

[3] This is the conclusion to which the main authorities of Finch's life and career point. These are the *Journals of the House of Commons*, Wood's *Athenae Oxonienses*, Burnet's *History* and Collin's *Peerage*.

candidates for preferment and, as his career well shows, Orlando Bridgeman was a man of principle and integrity. Traherne may well have won this wordly promotion on his merits; he took his B.D. in December 1669. One might wonder, though, why he chose to leave his obscure country parish for the house of the Lord Keeper of the Seal and 'the busie companies of men'. Would not the contemplative life be more easily followed in the seclusion and austerity of his life at Credinhill? Certainly Traherne has written of the dangers of comforts and wealth to the spiritual life; money, houses, lands, clothes, those indeed are dangerous, because 'Not the God of Nature but Sin only was the parent of them' (*Centuries*, III, 9).

> Riches are but tarnish and gilded vanities, honours are but airy and empty bubbles, affections are but winds . . . pleasures, yea all these, are but witches that draw and steal us away from God; dangerous allurements, interposing screens, unseasonable companions, counterfeit realities, honied poison, cumbersome distractions . . . (*Centuries*, IV, 89).

These words are not the language of the mystic, however, so much as the generalities of devotional admonition.

Traherne regards all conditions as offering potential good to the man who has become again as a child in simplicity of vision. The way to Felicity is the same for the poor as it is for the rich man. To enjoy the world depends not upon a change of outward circumstances, but upon a change in the self, an 'amendment' to use Traherne's term. Poverty, unless voluntary, may itself be a distraction to the realization of Felicity as much as riches; and conversely the houses of the great stand in as much need of hearing of the joys of felicity as those of the poor. In writing of felicity Traherne seems to give the word a variety of meanings which he does not separate clearly by means of the context in which it appears. The word ranges in meaning from the joyful sense of the immediate presence of God to something approaching the classical ideal of contentment, the good life.

It appears that no new appointment was made to the living at Credinhill until 1674 and the cause of the vacancy is then given to be the death of Thomas Traherne.[1] In the absence of further information it is not possible to say with certainty whether Traherne continued to enjoy the stipend of the living without making provision for its spiritual care. It appears that when the Bridgeman family visited Ted-

---

[1] *Institutions of the Diocese of Hereford* (A.D. 1539-1900) quoted by Gladys Wade, op. cit., p. 91.

dington, which they did whenever possible, Traherne acted as curate there although the living was nominally held by others.[1] However, there is no record that any similar arrangement was made at Credinhill. The existing parish registers there do not go further back than 1690, and there is no evidence in the annual transcripts in the Diocesan Registry at Hereford of any curate having been appointed. The transcripts for 1667 and 1668 were signed by Traherne. From 1669 to 1674 the signatures of churchwardens only appear.[2]

During the years of Traherne's chaplaincy the Bridgeman family lived either in their town house in the Strand, Essex House Court, or in their house in the High Street, Teddington. For the first years of Traherne's residence with them they lived for the most part in London. In the world of Restoration London the household must have provided an opportunity for study as well as meditation for Traherne. Sir Orlando is described as a learned and religious man and was interested in the thought of the Cambridge Platonists. He was a Cambridge man himself, and one of his chaplains, Hezekiah Burton, was a minor member of the Cambridge Platonists, a friend and correspondent of Henry More. According to Anthony à Wood's *Fasti Oxonienses*[3] Burton was still a chaplain to Sir Orlando in 1669. In this case he may well have been Traherne's colleague. A further point of contact with this group may possibly have been at St Lawrence Jewry where Whichcote (1610–83) was accustomed to preach at this time. Whether Traherne made any direct acquaintance with any of the more important figures of this movement or not, his own writings contain sufficient parallels with their work to warrant a discussion of them. I propose to do this in a later chapter.

Two years after Traherne's removal to London, Sir Orlando was deprived of his office and replaced by Shaftesbury. The Bridgemans withdrew to Teddington and Traherne went with them. Bridgeman's dismissal was on a point of conscience; he would not compromise his anti-Catholic position.[4] A year later, in November 1673, *Roman Forgeries* appeared. It was dedicated to Bridgeman to whom the 'Author

[1] Miss Wade mentions Bryan in 1668, and Graves in 1673, op. cit., p. 91.

[2] The yearly Bishop's transcripts of parish registers are generally signed by the Incumbent and Churchwardens.

[3] II, p. 186.

[4] Bishop Burnet, *The History of His Own Times* (ed. 1903), p. 114. Bridgeman refused to put the seal to the Declaration suspending the execution of all penal laws both against papists and nonconformists. This was the Declaration of Indulgence.

Devoteth his best Services and dedicateth the Use and Benefit of his Ensuing Labors'. The author's name does not appear; he is described simply as 'a Faithful Son of the Church of England'. The work itself is a piece of religious controversy, but by seventeenth-century standards comparatively restrained in tone. Scholarly and erudite, it is an attempt at historical criticism, to marshal the evidence to substantiate the charge made against the Church of Rome of using documents alleged not to be genuine; in brief, of tampering with the records of the Early Christian Church, the quasi-sacred writings of the Fathers, and canonical resolutions of the early Councils: 'I will ... keep close to Records ... such as Aposles, Canons, Decretal Epistles, and Ancient Councils; which they have either depraved by altering the Text, or falsified, as it were, by Whole-Sale, in the intire lump. . . . I shall not descend into the latter Ages, but keep within the compass of the first 420 years.' The work offers no evidence of Traherne's mysticism but it does reveal a power of judgement and analysis.

It has also, as Margoliouth points out, 'a distinct smell of the thesis'. The evidence here of intellectual ability is undoubted and is valuable to us in forming a balanced conception of Traherne. It reveals, too, an aspect of Traherne which places him as modern in his own times, a spirit of rational inquiry operating in matters of religious importance. As we shall see later, Traherne was far from depreciating the power of reason. He achieves a mystical enjoyment of God which he describes as a mystery; but he is not antagonistic to the tendencies of his time towards the rationalizing of religious belief. Reason, to Traherne, was a divine element in man and could lead him to the threshold of Felicity. It is the means by which a divine order is recognized in the universe. What we must note is that reason means more than ratiocination; it is not for Traherne simply the power of abstract thought. It is the image of Deity within us; the power which in harmony with the physical senses can lead to the knowledge of the truth: 'for here is victory and triumph over our lusts, that we might live the life of clear reason, in the fruition of all riches, honours, and pleasures, which are by wisdom to be seen, and by love to be enjoyed in the highest empire . . . in communion with all, by action and contemplation . . .' (*Centuries*, II, 99).

During the brief remainder of his patron's, and indeed of his own life at Teddington, Traherne must have been engaged in writing his lengthy work, *Christian Ethics;* and, no doubt, he continued the composition passage by passage of the *Centuries of Meditation*. Sir Orlando Bridgeman died in June 1674 after an illness of a little over a month. Traherne was a signatory of his will and of a codicil to it. In September of the same year Traherne was himself ill; ill enough to make a will of his own. He had little enough to dispose of, though the records show he owned five cottages[1] in Hereford which were not mentioned in the will, and what no doubt were a major item, 'All my books', he bequeathed to his brother Philip together with his 'best Hatt'. The will was made on 27 September 1674, and some short time afterwards, Traherne died. The precise date of his death is unknown, but Anthony à Wood records[2] that he was buried on 10 October beneath the reading desk in Teddington Church.

The editor of the *Contemplation* makes a fine tribute:

> He was a Divine of the Church of England, of a very comprehensive soul and very acute parts, so fully bent upon that Honourable function in which he was engaged, and so wonderfully transported with the excellency of these divine Laws, which are prescribed to us, and with those inexpressible felicities to which we are entitled by being created in the Divine Image, that he dwelt continually amongst these thoughts, with great delight and satisfaction, spending most of his time when at home, in digesting his notions of these things into writing, and was so full of them when abroad, that those who would converse with him, were forced to endure some discourse upon these subjects whether they had any sense of Religion or not.... His soul was of a more refined alloy and his judgement in discerning of things more solid and considerate than to be infected with that Leaven, and therefore became much in love with the beautiful order and primitive devotions of this our excellent Church.... He was a man of cheerful and sprightly temper, free from anything of the formality by which some great pretenders to Piety rather disparage or misrepresent true religion than recommend it; and therefore was very affable and pleasant in his conversation, ready to do all good offices to his friends, and charitable to the poor, almost beyond his ability. But being removed out of the country to the service of the late Lord Keeper Bridgeman, as his chaplain, he died young, and got early to those blissful mansions to which he at all times aspired.[3]

---

[1] After Traherne's death these five cottages became almshouses for the poor of All Souls' parish in Hereford.

[2] Op. cit., III, p. 106.

[3] From the Preface to *A Serious and Patheticall Contemplation* (1699).

CHAPTER II

The Spiritual Progress

i

TRAHERNE did not give his book the title *Centuries of Meditation*[1] and his main purpose would seem not to record his meditations but to instruct and encourage 'his friend' (almost certainly Mrs Hopton) in the way of enjoyment which he calls Felicity, 'to sing and rejoice and delight in God'. There are four *Centuries*, and ten sections of a fifth. The second *Century* follows on without any real break from the first, but the third has a separate character; it contains Traherne's account of his own progress in the enjoyment of Felicity. The fourth *Century* aims at setting out the 'principles' of Felicity, and the unfinished fifth is concerned with the mystical theme of God as both the Way towards, and the Object of, the seeker for Felicity, 'The Infinity of God is our Enjoyment.' The *Centuries* were probably written in the last years of Traherne's life during his time in London and Teddington, between 1669 and 1674.

ii

All appeared new, and strange at first, inexpressibly rare and delightful and beautiful. I was a little stranger, which at my entrance into the world was saluted and surrounded with innumerable joys. My knowledge was Divine. I knew by intuition those things which since my Apostasy, I collected again by the highest reason (*Centuries*, III, 2).

In these words Traherne points clearly to three phases in his mental and spiritual history. The first is that of an immediate and intuitive apprehension, a sense of wonder at the beauty of the world:

The corn was orient and immortal wheat, which never should be reaped, nor was ever sown. I thought it had stood from everlasting to everlasting. The dust and stones of the street were as precious as gold: the gates were at first the end of the world. The green trees when I saw them first through one

---

[1] This title was written in a hand which, though possibly seventeenth century, is not thought to be Traherne's.

of the gates transported and ravished me, their sweetness and unusual beauty made my heart leap, and almost mad with ecstasy, they were such strange and wonderful things (*Centuries*, III, 3).

This experience Traherne describes as a 'pure and virgin' apprehension, the shining of a 'first Light' in 'primitive and innocent clarity'. These apprehensions were 'natural, and unmixed' (*Centuries*, III, 8). Traherne writes of them as belonging to his infancy; their brilliance comes from the 'Light which shined in my Infancy' (*Centuries*, III, 7). 'Certainly Adam in Paradise had not more sweet and curious apprehensions of the world, than I when I was a child' (*Centuries*, III, 1). The comparison to the Garden of Eden continues:

> I saw all in the peace of Eden; Heaven and Earth did sing my Creator's praises, and could not make more melody to Adam, than to me. All Time was Eternity, and a perpetual Sabbath. Is it not strange that an infant should be heir of the whole World, and see those mysteries which the books of the learned never unfold? (*Centuries*, III, 2).

This vision of perfection which Traherne enjoyed is an image of the pre-lapsarian world; and the references to the Garden of Eden are significant. These pure and virgin apprehensions belong to a state which precedes the knowledge of good and evil. They belong to the world of infancy not only in time but in quality. This sense of glory is not the result of disciplined endeavour, or profound meditation. It belongs to a situation; it is incidental to a particular set of circumstances. As such, therefore, it is different from the later experience of Traherne's life in which a comparable sense of exaltation is achieved through knowledge and through illumination and which is independent of the circumstances of time and place. The purity and splendour of the world that the child Traherne saw were so because he was a child; they are involved in his childhood and are not separable from the limitations of childhood. In other words this vision of the world is not to be taken necessarily as a vision of reality, and therefore I hesitate to call such experience mystical in the fullest sense of the term. The vision of the child is of a world not separable from itself; the excitement of Traherne's description expresses the sense of triumph in possession which accompanies the extension of experience in a child's life. The world he saw was glorious and magnificent, but above all it was his, a part of himself, his private property: 'The Streets were mine, the temple was mine, the people were mine, their clothes and gold and silver were mine, as much as their sparkling eyes, fair skins and ruddy faces. The skies were mine, and so were the sun and moon and stars, and all the World was mine; and I the only spectator and enjoyer of it' (*Centuries*, III, 3). This is a statement of an experience felt to be unique; it makes no assertion of the presence of a transcendent reality. It has the authenticity of an intense and intuitive apprehension. By contrast the sentence, 'My knowledge was Divine,' stands in a certain isolation. I do not feel that Traherne is behind it in the same way as in the later passage: 'The corn was orient and immortal wheat, which never should be reaped. . . .' When Traherne wrote of these intuitive childhood experiences that 'My knowledge was Divine' he is including his subsequent experience in what he says; it is essentially a reflective statement. It has, that is, a reference to the time when he wrote it as well as to the events about which it was written. It is not a re-creation of an experience so much as a comment upon that experience and an interpretation of it. The child who apprehends these things is not aware of reality as divine or indeed as not divine. It is the man writing in later years who makes the judgement, and the intervening years have taken part in the forming of the conclusion.

To deny a mystical status 'in the fullest sense of the term' to these childhood experiences of Traherne demands an attempt at defining this fullest sense. The following passage is relevant here:

> The mystic experience ends with the words: 'I live, yet not I, but God in me'. This feeling of identification, which is the term of mystical activity, has a very important significance. In its early stages the mystic consciousness feels the Absolute in opposition to the Self . . . as mystic activity goes on, it tends to abolish this opposition. . . . When it has reached its term the consciousness finds itself possessed by the sense of a Being at one and the same time greater than the Self and identical with it: great enough to be God, intimate enough to be me.[1]

This account accords with much that Traherne has written in the *Centuries of Meditation*, but the childhood experiences lie outside it. The sense of perfection that characterizes them in Traherne's descriptions, the sense of timelessness, belongs to a state prior to the consciousness of an opposition between the absolute and the self, and it is with this awareness that the mystical experience can properly be said to begin.

How, then, are we to consider this early ecstatic enjoyment of Traherne of the 'strange and wonderful beauty of the world and the

---

[1] E. Recejac, *Les Fondements de la Connaissance Mystique* (London, 1899), p. 45.

creatures in it'? In the first place, the experience provides an image of the paradise 'to the enjoyment of which every man is naturally born' (*Centuries*, III, 5). In the second place, its context indicates an important means by which this felicity is to be attained: 'all our thoughts must be infant-like and clear; the powers of our soul free from the leaven of this world, and disentangled from men's conceits and customs' (*Centuries*, III, 5). We must become 'as it were but little children' (ibid.), taking on those qualities of pure perception and absolute belief which the adult mind attributes to the child. The purity resides in the perception of objects as they really are; the child's clear vision will 'let a man see those objects truly that are before it' (ibid.). The child sees the world with the same eyes as Adam; 'Ambitions, trades, luxuries, inordinate affections, casual and accidental riches invented since the fall, would be gone, and only those things appear, which did to Adam in Paradise, in the same light and in the same colours' (ibid.). What the child experiences is an image of the Felicity to attain which is the proper end of human life for Traherne; the mode of experience of the child is a means to this end. In all this Traherne assumes that a child really does 'see those objects that are truly before it' as they really are. The vision of the child is, for him, the vision of things as they are in reality. In other words the child becomes a symbol in Traherne's thoughts, the symbol of direct and immediate knowledge of reality.

The childhood experience is equated with the 'peace of Eden; . . . The Estate of Innocence' (*Centuries*, III, 2). The identification is significant. The world of Traherne's childhood is a world without knowledge of good and evil:

> My very ignorance was advantageous. . . . All things were spotless and pure and glorious; yea, and infinitely mine and joyful and precious. I knew not that there were any sins, or complaints or vices. All tears and quarrels were hidden from mine eyes. . . . I knew nothing of sickness or death or rents or exaction, either for tribute or bread. In the absence of these I was entertained like an Angel with the works of God in their splendour and glory, I saw all in the Peace of Eden (ibid.).

We see, then, that this happiness is involved with an unawareness of certain aspects of existence. As such it is not to be identified with the mystical vision. It remains an image of Felicity, an indication of the experience that can be achieved. It is not, however, the same thing as that Felicity. As we shall see later, the Felicity that Traherne achieves

c

is not simply the ecstasy that was part of his childhood and which shares the qualities and limitations of childhood. It is an experience which does not depend upon the absence of pain, anxiety or sin, or upon an unawareness of the unpleasant and uncomfortable aspects of life, but which is based upon an increased sensitivity, a heightened awareness of the 'goodness' of things, a 'secret strength',[1] a power of taking 'delight in calamities and distresse for God's sake' (*Centuries*, IV, 91). Instead of the emphasis on the sense of possession of the beauty of the world as an extension of the self, there is to be seen, in the expression of Traherne's adult vision, an emphasis on outward action and on active meditation: 'The soul is made for action, and cannot rest till it be employed. Idleness is its rust, Unless it will up and think and taste and see, all is in vain.' 'If you will be lazy and not meditate, you lose all' (*Centuries*, IV, 95). By comparison, the childhood experience is passive, something which cannot be helped, given the particular circumstances of temperament and environment. The adult vision is more positive; even so, something of the childlike quality remains. We do not know to what depths Traherne's knowledge of good and evil reached, if it went deep at all. But with this vision, 'a soul loves freely and purely of its own self, with God's love, things that seem incapable of love, naught and evil' (*Centuries*, IV, 87). As it is written this is different from the childhood vision described in the first sections of the Third *Century*. There is no indication there of the conception of a love which can penetrate and transcend the whole range of experience 'freely and purely of its own self', nor indeed would we expect to find such a conception.

I conclude therefore that the ecstatic enjoyment of Traherne's childhood vision is an image of the happiness which is the consequence of mystical illumination, but that we should hesitate to describe this enjoyment as itself mystical. Alcohol or hypnosis may produce similar effects; but we would not describe such experiences therefore as mystical. It would seem that the fundamental fact of this discussion is that the nature and quality of the mystical experience is determined by the means through and by which it is realized. The stages of the way make the mystic as well as the Felicity which crowns his journey.

These 'pure and virgin apprehensions' which Traherne possessed 'from the womb' are described by him as 'the divine light wherewith I was born' (*Centuries*, III, 1). He remembered them in later years as

[1] *Centuries*, IV, 97.

'the greatest gifts' God's 'wisdom could bestow, for without them all other gifts had been dead and vain. They are unattainable by book, and therefore I will teach them by experience' (*Centuries*, III, 1). It was Nature, 'the works of God in their splendour and glory', which was bathed in this unearthly light and yet which seemed at the same time the source of wonder. There is nothing here of the conception of original sin as infecting the natural world of sense perception. The account which the adult thinker gives of his childhood intuitions accords with the characteristic movement towards enlightenment which the seventeenth century was witnessing. Traherne was giving evidence of what, for instance, the Cambridge Platonists were demonstrating by argument, that there was a natural goodness in nature, both in human nature and the world in which we live: 'Natural things are glorious, and to know them glorious. . . . The riches of Nature are our Souls and Bodies, with all their faculties, senses and endowments' (*Centuries*, III, 9). Although Traherne does not insist that Eden was a place or the Fall an historical event, seeing them rather as images of a state of being or a spiritual process, he does not deny a Fall of Man. He writes of the two worlds, one made by God, the other by men: 'That made by God was great and beautiful. Before the Fall it was Adam's joy and the Temple of his Glory. That made by men is a Babel of Confusions: invented Riches, Pomps and Vanities, brought in by Sin' (*Centuries*, I, 7). The fall of man involves the loss of the enjoyment of this great and beautiful world; it is an event which takes place in the life of the individual. Traherne says little of the Fall as an aboriginal calamity as a result of which man is utterly depraved.[1] It is for him the eclipsing of the pure and unmixed vision of the child, and of the natural man. Man falls from the estate of innocence because he turns from nature to a world of artificiality and invention. He turns from the revelation of the sun and stars to the 'strange riches of invention' (*Centuries*, III, 9) and these are 'gold, silver, houses, lands, clothes', the creatures of 'art and error' (*Centuries*, III, 9). The natural man to Traherne is as Adam was, and the natural man is compared with the wonder of the child and the unsophisticated savage: 'They that go naked and drink water and live upon roots are like Adam, or Angels in comparison of us. . . . I am sure those barbarous people that go

---

[1] In addition to the reference already given I find two further instances: 'Yet is all our corruption derived from Adam: in as much as all the evil examples and inclinations of the world arise from his sin' (*Centuries*, III, 8), and 'We have his fall . . . original and actual' (*Centuries*, III, 43).

naked, come nearer to Adam, God and Angels. . . .' (*Centuries*, III, 12).
Indeed nowhere in Traherne do we find any great awareness of the
gulf which separates the natural man from the spiritual man.

The fall of man is re-enacted in Traherne's own history; he calls it
'my Apostasy' (*Centuries*, III, 2) and it marks the second phase of his
spiritual progress. The childhood vision of the 'peace of Eden', the
ecstatic joy in the 'boys and girls tumbling in the street, and playing'
as 'moving jewels' (*Centuries*, III, 3) is lost; the 'first Light which
shined in my Infancy in its primitive and innocent clarity was totally
eclipsed' (*Centuries*, III, 7). The eclipse came not suddenly but by
degrees, 'and at last the celestial, great and stable treasures to which I
was born, as wholly forgotten as if they had never been' (*Centuries*,
III, 7). The reasons for this loss lie in the growing acquaintance with
the world of men, in the corrupting influence of 'the dirty devices of
this world' (*Centuries*, III, 3). This corruption is caused 'by the customs
and manners of men, . . . by the impetuous torrent of wrong desires
in all others whom I saw or knew . . . by a whole sea of other matters
and concernments that covered and drowned it (*sc.* the Light): finally
by the evil influence of a bad education that did not foster and cherish
it' (*Centuries*, III, 7). The light could not exist by itself and of itself in
the child's mind; it was the product of a situation and changed as the
situation changed. The emphasis of Traherne's words points to the
effect of a change of environment; it is the influence of others which
is blamed for the loss of the first light. It is because others do not speak
of or value like experiences that it fades in Traherne's mind: 'All men's
thoughts and words were about other matters. They all prized new
things which I did not dream of. . . . I was weak, and easily guided by
their example; ambitious also, and desirous to approve myself unto
them. And finding no one syllable in any man's mouth of those things,
by degrees they vanished . . .' (*Centuries*, III, 7).

The 'fall', then, which is enacted in his own being does not result
from anything more sinful in himself than a propensity to be too easily
influenced by others. It is not the consequence of a primordial act
through which humanity is inevitably infected with sin; 'our misery
proceedeth ten thousand times more from the outward bondage of
opinion and custom, than from any inward corruption or depravation
of Nature' (*Centuries*, III, 8). Sin is not so much original, that is, as the
consequence of the plastic nature of the child's being: 'An empty book
is like an infant's soul, in which anything may be written. It is capable
of all things, but containeth nothing' (*Centuries*, I, 1). It is evil example

which corrupts; if the growing influence on his nature had been of another kind, Traherne says, his vision of the

> Skies in their Magnificence
> The lovly lively Air[1]
> (*Wonder*, l. 10)

would not have been lost 'had any man spoken of it, it had been the most easy thing in the world, to have taught me, and to have made me believe that Heaven and Earth was God's House, and that he gave it me. ... From whence I clearly find how docible our Nature is in natural things, were it rightly entreated' (*Centuries*, III, 8). Man's nature is not so much corrupt as corruptible; it is not basically imperfect, to be redeemed only by grace. Traherne thinks always, and his thought is the reflection of his individual experience, of the nature of man and the world of nature as essentially good in their 'simple state'; the senses when they are unclouded, unobscured by custom or artificiality are direct avenues to the Light which it is the end of human life to know:

> For simple Sense
> Is Lord of all created Excellence[2]
> (*The Preparative*, l. 39-40)

Traherne's apostasy as he terms it, his fall from the estate of innocence, is the result of the disruption of the harmony, a defect in awareness of the true nature of his happiness which leads to the substitution of wrong objects for the proper object of contemplation; and the wrong objects are those that lead away from the highest satisfaction. It is a consequence of his childish state in which intuition exists without a corresponding power of intelligence. In this sense evil for Traherne is not real; it is the result of an imperfect realization of the world and of the nature of man. It lies in an insensitivity, in a refusal to see: 'No man can sin that clearly seeth the beauty of God's face' (*Centuries*, II, 97). One must remember always that Traherne's writings are based on his own experience and that which seems to be a generalization is a record of individual knowledge. This reminder is, I think, important. Isolated from this context much of what Traherne wrote might be taken for an expansive, almost eighteenth-century optimism.

[1] Traherne, *Centuries, Poems and Thanksgivings*, ed. H. M. Margoliouth (Oxford, 1958), vol. II, p. 8. (All references to the poems are to this edition.)
[2] Op. cit., p. 22.

The 'simple state' is that of the child's intuition, but that is essentially the child's vision of the world and in any case is recorded in recollection. We can never be sure how far the adult's memory of his childhood is true to the experience of childhood, or to what extent a contribution is made by maturity in the very process of writing down the memories of those experiences. I have hesitated to describe the first phase as mystical therefore on the grounds that the childhood experience is by its very circumstances of a subjectivity so inevitable that it cannot be properly discussed as such. A mystical experience is a direct experience of a reality which transcends the individual. Traherne himself claims this quality for his childhood vision, but as I have suggested it would be truer to say that these 'natural and unmixed apprehensions' represent less a vision of transcendent reality than the ecstasy of innocence and inexperience. They indicate the intensity of the mystic's joy, its ecstatic quality, rather than the distinctive quality of mysticism which is that it is a direct experience of an absolute reality existing independently of the individual. I take further support for this position from what may be inferred of this second stage which we are discussing, Traherne's 'apostasy'. Indeed, this very apostasy, this loss of the vision of the splendour and magnificence of the world and the creatures in it, is a step forward towards the beginning of the mystical way proper. The loss of the first light is in a sense necessary for the complete awareness of the later experience, the Felicity which is to come. The eclipsing of the true objects was for Traherne the means of knowing what those true objects really were; by their very absence they became known: 'The Heavens and the Sun and the Stars . . . disappeared, and were no more unto me than the bare walls. So that the strange riches of man's invention quite overcame the riches of Nature, being learned more laboriously and in the second place' (*Centuries*, III, 10). The step became a step forward when 'the strange riches of man's invention' were found to be less satisfying than 'the riches of Nature' which they replaced. The distinction began in Traherne's mind to develop between 'natural things' and what he called 'preternatural'[1] things, 'gold, silver, houses, lands, clothes' and the prizing of these things as valuable in themselves.

At what time in his life Traherne realized that the objects which had eclipsed the first light, and which were the objects which form the normal preoccupations of men, were illusory and unable to satisfy the inner demands of his being we cannot say. The recording of this realization is obviously later than its occurrence:

[1] *Centuries*, III, 9, i.e. artificial.

Being swallowed up therefore in the miserable gulf of idle talk and worthless vanities, thenceforth I lived among dreams and shadows, like a prodigal son feeding upon husks with swine. A comfortless wilderness full of thorns and troubles of the world was, or worse: a waste place covered with idleness and play, and shops, and markets, and taverns. As for Churches they were things I did not understand, and schools were a burden: so that there was nothing in the world worth the having, or enjoying, but my game and sport, which also was a dream, and being passed wholly forgotten. So that I had utterly forgotten all goodness, bounty, comfort, and glory: which things are the very brightness of the Glory of God: for lack of which therefore He was unknown (*Centuries*, III, 14).

The emphatic rhythms of this passage convey the vividness of his memory of this nadir of experience; the strength of the recollection is evidence of the intensity of the original feeling. The first light is completely forgotten and the very objects which replaced it have themselves become unreal. The world of men had influenced the growing child: 'I was weak and easily guided by their example; ambitious also, and desirous to approve myself unto them.' Through weakness of will the young Traherne had turned to the world of conventional mundane civilization, in the same way as

> only foolish men
> Grown mad with customary Folly
> Which doth increase their Wants, so dote
> As when they elder grow they then
> Such Baubles chiefly note:
> More Fools at Twenty Years than Ten.[1]
> (*The Apostacy*, ll. 49–54)

Yet this very world had itself become profoundly unsatisfactory and meaningless. He had reached now a point where the sense of pointlessness in life, 'that the World was . . . empty . . . vain and forlorn' (*Centuries*, III, 15), became intolerable: 'Dissatisfied with my present state,' he writes, 'sometimes in the midst of these dreams, I should come a little to myself, so far as to feel I wanted something . . . to long after an unknown happiness' (*Centuries*, III, 15). The realization of the world of human society as a waste place, a comfortless wilderness, gives rise to an impulse to seek for a meaning, to find the reality which was missing. This is the point of advance; the determination to find a solution which should be real. The sense of emptiness generates a desire to achieve a substantial happiness. Another advance is to be noted here:

[1] Op. cit., pp. 96–7.

there is a growing differentiation between the self and that unknown which lies outside it. The description of the early ecstasies shows in their very expression a repeated and emphatic sense of possession: 'The streets were mine, the temple were mine, the people were mine, their clothes and gold and silver were mine . . .'—it is himself which is the chief focus; the repetition of 'mine' is significant. It is not the reality of other things, the sense that there is a truth existing absolutely outside the self which arouses these delights. The objects of this enjoyment are aspects of himself, incorporated in his own being. There is no sense of any gap between the self and the not-self. But now with this sense of loss there is to be seen also a growing sense of self, as a separate and distinct being: 'Yet sometimes . . . I should come a little to myself, . . . sometimes I should be alone, and without employment, when suddenly my Soul would return to itself' (*Centuries*, III, 17). In a world of shadows, in which there was nothing 'worth the having or enjoying', this growing realization of his own self and its questionings becomes a basis of certainty. The self is real; this is one conviction and the other is that there is a 'something', unknown, existing outside the self, which will supply a happiness and purpose to a life which was empty and without meaning. Yet not only was it the unsatisfactory nature of his world which impelled Traherne to look for the unknown Felicity; he was prompted also 'by a real whispering instinct of Nature' (*Centuries*, III, 16).

This reference to instinctive promptings is important; he refers a little later to 'new and more vigorous desires after that bliss which Nature whispered and suggested to me' (*Centuries*, III, 22). I take this to mark the ending of this second phase of his spiritual life. The third phase is the progress by means of 'the highest reason' to the Felicity of which the intuitions of childhood had already given an indication and which, in Traherne's terms, were identical with it. I prefer to make a distinction and regard this third phase as the mystical period of his life. However, before I proceed to a consideration of this phase there remain still certain points to discuss in this second phase, that of his apostasy. Traherne speaks of the whispering instincts of Nature urging him to seek the as yet unknown Felicity; unknown, that is, because the first light has been and still remains eclipsed. He is quite sure that this good exists but he does not yet know what it is, and his conviction is based on 'instinct' rather than on reason. It is possible here that, although the records of Traherne's spiritual progress in his prose writings are contained in the *Third* and *Fourth Century*, the words of the opening sections of the *First Century* refer also to this period of his spiritual life;

> for though it be a maxim in the schools *that there is no Love of a thing unknown,* yet I have found that things unknown have a secret influence on the soul, and like the centre of the earth unseen violently attract it. We love we know not what, and therefore everything allures us. As iron at a distance is drawn by the loadstone, there being some invisible communications between them, so is there in us a world of Love to somewhat, though we know not what in the world that should be. There are invisible ways of conveyance by which some great thing doth touch our souls, and by which we tend to it. Do you not feel yourself drawn by the expectation and desire of some Great Thing?' (*Centuries*, I, 2).

This passage points to the meanings which we must give to Traherne's use of the word 'instinct'. It refers to a total situation, the impact of a cause existing outside the individual with a potentiality within the individual. This 'instinct of Nature' is not wholly within the self as an inherited power like the ability to see or the desire for food. On the contrary Traherne held that the infant's soul is 'capable of all things, but containeth nothing' (*Centuries*, I, 1). What Traherne is implying is that the desire for Felicity is caused by the actual existence of this 'Great Thing'. In other words the desire would not exist were it not for the real existence of the object of this desire. The presence of the impulse to find Felicity is a guarantee of the existence of Felicity. The 'instinct of Nature', as Traherne terms it, refers then to the reaction of the individual to an objective reality. Nature whispers and suggests, as it seems, because his individual self is not yet attuned to the reality which is calling. The full potentialities have not yet been realized, either of himself or of the total situation. When this occurs the whispers become indomitable affirmations, or, as it could be put with equal truth, full realization occurs because the whispers are accepted with full authority. Nature in this context seems to refer to a force existing outside himself, a reality breaking into the 'comfortless wilderness full of thorns and troubles'.

What indeed we are witnessing, expressed in terms of Traherne's own experience, is a re-statement, as a fact of religious experience and not as an abstraction, of one of the dominant ideas of medieval scholasticism, that like causes beget like effects.[1] The very desire for

---

[1] 'What ever exists in the effect must have existed . . . in its cause.' Carré, *Phases of Thought in England* (Oxford, 1949), p. 138. See also E. Gilson, *The Spirit of Medieval Philosophy* (London, 1936), for many instances of this idea.

Felicity argues that there is a Felicity. The desire could not exist unless there was a cause similar in its nature to the desire. It is the very existence of Felicity which causes the desire for it. I do not suggest that Traherne consciously formulated this idea under the influence of Aristotelian scholastic philosophy. (He was certainly acquainted with the thought of the 'schools' and, as I have noted, there are echoes of Aquinas in his phrases.) The process was not a logical one. Traherne was writing the *Centuries* some years after the date of the spiritual events he records. In the interval he became actually aware of the Felicity which at the time of which he writes was unknown to him. In other words his own subsequent experience had fully shown that there was a Felicity corresponding to the whispering suggestions that had come to him at the time of his apostasy. This Felicity was not simply a temporary reaction of an individual to a particular cause; it was a consequence of the experience of a timeless reality. That is, the possibility of its experience was always present, present at the time of his ignorance of it.

That Felicity was unknown does not destroy its power of action, but the individual person has to amend himself, to take positive steps to meet the 'great thing' to which he is drawn. He is drawn to the things unknown because there is in himself that 'by which we tend to it'. The influence on the soul is exerted secretly even when that soul is in a state of apostasy, of ignorance of any reality. Here Traherne is again writing of an original experience seen against a context defined and enlarged by his subsequent experience. It is on the grounds of his later and fuller knowledge that he asserts the 'whispering instinct of Nature' was real. Traherne's criterion of 'the real' was not that of logical consistency but that of actual and individual experience.

In summary, this as yet vaguely apprehended distinction between the individual self and some 'great thing' felt to be separate from and superior to the self marks both the end of Traherne's period of 'apostasy' and the beginning of the third phase of his spiritual history. This third phase is the 'collection' again of the supreme satisfaction of the vision of the world as divine. Traherne writes 'again' because to him this Felicity is identical with the childhood *as he remembers it*. This supreme experience was not achieved 'till a long time afterwards' (*Centuries*, III, 22). It was a process consummated finally by the 'emanations of the highest reason'. Traherne distinguishes in this way the means by which this final knowledge is attained.

The 'highest reason' is clearly meant to be distinct from 'intuition' and different also from 'ordinary reason'. If, however, to Traherne both intuition and the highest reason lead to an identical experience which is the knowledge of divine reality, there must be at some stage some ground of similarity between them that is not shared by the ordinary or normal reason. I suggest that Traherne is using the words 'the highest reason' in the sense in which the term 'intellect' is used in scholastic philosophy. Certainly it may be argued that his 'highest reason' is no doubt the *'in summa Rationis arce'* which he attributes, wrongly, to Plato in the 60th Meditation of the *Third Century*, and he is certainly in touch with the movements of Renaissance Platonism as I shall point out later. However, what is most characteristic of Traherne's mystical writings inclines more, I think, to the medieval realism of the scholastics,[1] and, in particular that of Aquinas. Traherne sees the world of sensible appearances as necessary for the knowledge of the very experience of God. The senses are the means to the experience of Felicity which Traherne, as we shall see later, equates with the full knowledge of divine reality; Felicity is 'immediately near to the very gates of our senses' (*Centuries*, I, 23). The object which is to be realized as the goal of the mystical journey is beyond the categories of sense, but all the various powers of the human organism can lead to that object; 'Let heaven and earth, men and angels, God and his creatures be always within us, that is *in our sight, in our sense,*[2] in our love and esteem' (*Centuries*, I, 100). The senses are closely linked with the understanding; without sensible objects 'Your thoughts and inclinations pass on, and are unperceived but by their objects are discerned to be present: being illuminated by them' (*Centuries*, II, 78). Sensible objects are necessary for the understanding to be effective at all (*Centuries*, II, 78). Finally, the understanding is a mode of participation in the life of other beings: 'You shall be present with them (*sc.* created things) in your understanding. You shall be in them to the very centre and they in you. . . . An Act of the Understanding is the presence of the Soul' (*Centuries*, II, 76). My point is this: all that Traherne has written in these few extracts (which could be easily multiplied) is thoroughly in the spirit of medieval scholastic philosophy. For instance, Etienne Gilson writes of St Thomas Aquinas: 'far from agreeing with Plato that the proper

---

[1] Cf. 'The creatures of this visible world signify the invisible attributes of God, because God is the source, model and last end of every creature and because every effect points to its cause, every image to its model, every road to its goal.' St Bonaventure, *Itinerarium mentis in Deum*, I, 14.

[2] My italics.

and natural object of our intellect is the intelligible Idea, to which we should endeavour painfully to rise by a violent effort of detachment from sense, he declares himself at one with Aristotle—and with experience—in affirming that, in this life, we can form no concept unless first we have received a sense impression, nor even return later on to this concept without turning to the images that sense has left behind in the imagination. There is therefore a natural relation, an essential proportion, between the human intellect and the nature of material things. . . .'[1]

Traherne's conception of the understanding as that by which you may 'be present now with all the creatures among which you live' (*Centuries*, II, 76) is the same as that of Aquinas: 'The intellect grasps "being"; it can somehow assimilate all that is: *intellectus potest quodammodo omnia fieri*.'[2] Aquinas held that the divine reality is not entirely alien to the human intellect. Certainly it is beyond its reach, but only because it is infinite, not because it is formally unknowable: '*divina substantia non sic est extra faculatem intellectus creati; quasi aliquid omnino extraneum ab ipso*'.[3] I suggest from this that when Traherne wrote of collecting again 'by the highest reason' those things—the innumerable joys with which his entrance into the world was saluted—which once he knew by intuition, the common meaning which is shared by the reason and intuition is that of the Thomist meaning of intellect. This is not to identify the highest reason with intuition; it is to remark that that part of their meanings which is possessed by both consists in the sense of participating in, of becoming one with some other being. I prefer therefore to remove the 'highest reason' in this context, which is that of Traherne the mystic, from an exclusively Platonic setting. There is, as I shall point out later, another context, that of Traherne's Platonism which I consider to be on a different level from his essential mysticism. There is a further point to be noted in discussing the meaning to be given to Traherne's 'highest reason' and which places it in a different field from the geometric reason of some of his contemporaries. The experience of Felicity, 'These liquid, clear satisfactions', are described by him as 'emanations of the highest reason' (*Centuries*, III, 22). The *New English Dictionary* is helpful in its comment here; 'emanation' in the seventeenth century, in the sense of that which proceeds from a

---

[1] E. Gilson, *The Spirit of Medieval Philosophy* (London, 1936), p. 249.

[2] M. de Wulf, *Philosophy and Civilisation in the Middle Ages* (Princeton, 1922), p. 182.

[3] Aquinas, *Cont. Gent.*, III, 54, ad Rationes.

source, is associated particularly with theories that regard either the universe as a whole, or the spiritual aspect of it, as deriving its existence from the essence of God and not from an act of creation out of nothing.[1]

This is important in forming a judgement of Traherne's meaning for highest reason. It is a further instance of a link with scholastic ideas. The highest reason is clearly more than ratiocination, than intellectual analysis; it is the power which leads Traherne to the very threshold of the mystical vision, to the full understanding which transcends all other knowledge. If it is the emanations of the highest reason which bring about the realization of God and if emanation has the meaning of that which proceeds from a divine source, then, logically one might suppose that the highest reason itself is of the essence of God. Furthermore Traherne speaks always of the highest reason or the 'life of clear reason' impersonally as if it were more than a characteristic of an individual like the possession of intelligence or sensitivity to certain sounds or colours. To live the 'life of clear reason' seems plainly to be on a different level of meaning from 'to have a good brain' or 'a good ear'. In other words the highest reason is conceived as a reality existing apart from individual consciousness of it; the individual may, after long effort and discipline, participate in this life or he may never do so and it will remain for him an unrealized possibility. By 'the highest reason' I take it that Traherne had in mind the power, always possible to human persons but only rarely achieved, of knowing truth, objective reality. Furthermore to know reality in this sense means to understand it, that is to share its being, to become one with it. The mystical advance which forms the third and final phase of Traherne's spiritual life proceeds by the agency of 'the highest reason'; but though this may reveal the truth and reveal him as a participant in this truth it would still fall short of the final mystical experience. For this to take place the highest reason is not enough; it must be superseded by the love of reality: 'For God gave man an endless intellect to see all things, and a proneness to covet them, because they are His treasures' (*Centuries*, III, 42), and Traherne proceeds to enumerate the qualities by which man may proceed to the highest good; and the climax is reached by 'a power of admiring, loving and prizing, that seeing the beauty and goodness of God, he might be united to it for evermore' (*Centuries*, III, 42).

[1] Cf. H. More, *Poems* (1647), 279:

> 'Man's soul's not by Creation
> Wherefore let't be by Emanation.'

CHAPTER III

The Limitations of Traherne's Mystical Experience

I HAVE defined the ending of Traherne's period of 'apostasy' as marking at the same moment the beginning of the final phase of his spiritual progress. This point is determined by his awareness of a longing for an unknown happiness, 'a desire of which I flagrantly burned' (*Centuries*, III, 38); 'happiness was that I thirsted after' (*Centuries*, III, 39). His desire was so intense for this unknown happiness that he was convinced that it came from outside himself, from 'Nature'. He was not yet aware of its cause as Divine, only at first as something not himself, 'the very force wherewith we covet it supplying the place of understanding' (*Centuries*, III, 56). He called this urgent desire for Felicity an instinct because, like hunger and thirst, it was beyond conscious control. He recorded his awareness on a particular occasion of an isolation, a sense of loneliness in the universe, a sudden terror of the stars;

> in a lowering and sad evening, being alone in the field, when all things were dead and quiet, a certain want and horror fell upon me, beyond imagination. The unprofitableness and silence of the place dissatisfied me; its wideness terrified me; from the utmost ends of the earth fears surrounded me. How did I know but dangers might suddenly arise from the East, and invade me from the unknown regions beyond the seas? I was a weak and little child, and had forgotten there was a man alive in the earth. Yet something also of hope and expectation conforted me from every border. This taught me that I was concerned in all the world: and that in the remotest borders the causes of peace delight me, and the beauties of the earth when seen were made to entertain me: that I was made to hold a communion with the secrets of Divine Providence in all the world (*Centuries*, III, 23).

A similar though less complex experience lies at the centre of the poem *Solitude*:[1]

> I do believ
> The Ev'ning being shady and obscure,
> The very Silence did me griev,

---

[1] Op. cit., p. 98.

And sorrow more procure:
A secret Want
Did make me think my Fortune scant.
I was so blind, I could not find my Health,
No Joy mine Ey could espy, nor Wealth.

Nor could I ghess
What kind of thing I long'd for: But that
Did somewhat lack of Blessedness,
Beside the Earth and Sky,
I plainly found;
It griev'd me much, I felt a Wound
Perplex me sore; Yet what my Store should be
I did not know, nothing would shew to me.

Ye sullen Things!
Ye dumb, ye silent Creatures, and unkind!
How can I call you Pleasant Springs
Unless ye eas my Mind!
Will ye not speak
What 'tis I want, nor Silence break?
O pity me, at least point out my Joy:
Som Kindness shew to me, altho a Boy.

They silent stood;
Nor Earth, nor Woods, nor Hills, nor Brooks, nor Skies,
Would tell me where the hidden Good,
Which I did long for, lies:
The shady Trees,
The Ev'ning dark, the humming Bees,
The chirping Birds, mute Springs and Fords, conspire,
To giv no Answer unto my Desire. (ll. 25-56)

Both the prose and the poetry express the sense of profound dis-
satisfaction at the absence in external nature of an object adequate to
the urgent desire within him; yet both extracts express also the sense
that such an object does actually exist. There is a tension, a sense of
expectation, an almost intolerable waiting for the communication that
is felt to be imminent but is not yet intelligible. The prose goes further
than the poetry; the poetry expresses the immediate sense of baffled
hopelessness linked with fear at not finding a reality and at the same
time convinced of its existence. The prose extract is another example
of a mixed record; the actual experience is recorded together with a

comment on the meaning of the experience: 'This taught me that I was concerned in all the world: and that in the remotest borders the causes of peace delight me, and the beauties of the earth when seen were made to entertain me: that I was made to hold a communion with the secrets of Divine Providence in all the World.'

The content of the actual experience is analysed into its effects. The nature of these is seen to be two-fold. What is first felt to be fear and doubt, the apprehension of 'unknown modes of being', is also 'the clear assurance of treasure everywhere, God's care and love, His goodness, wisdom, and power, His presence and watchfulness in all the end of the earth' (*Centuries*, III, 23). The sense of terror that the universe exists as an alien, even hostile power apart from himself, the sense of his complete isolation,—for I take this to be the force of the words 'I . . . had forgotten there was a man alive in the earth'—is mingled with 'something also of hope and expectation' which came as an effective comfort. The fear, while remaining fear, is also the ground for rejoicing. This is the meaning of the experience as it seemed to Traherne on reflection. I say this because the words 'this taught me that I was concerned in all the world' seem to point to a later realization. The actual experience was complex, and it was only on analysis made in the light of later knowledge that the sense of isolation was realized as having contained within it its own antidote. Traherne at the time of this experience was not fully aware of its implications for him; at the time when he wrote of it, though, he was in a position to assess its meaning.

The event recorded in this passage from the *Centuries*, and the prose seems much more actual and immediate than the poem, is comparable to the experience recounted in another record of 'Childhood and Schooltime', Book I of Wordsworth's *Prelude*:

> lustily
> I dipped my oars into the silent lake,
> And, as I rose upon the stroke, my boat
> Went heaving through the water like a swan;
> When, from behind that craggy steep till then
> The horizon's bound, a huge peak, black and huge,
> As if with voluntary power instinct,
> Upreared its head. I struck and struck again,
> And growing still in stature the grim shape
> Towered up between me and the stars, and still,
> For so it seemed, with purpose of its own
> And measured motion like a living thing
> Strode after me. With trembling oars I turned,

And through the silent water stole my way
. . . . but after I had seen
That spectacle, for many days, my brain
Worked with a dim and undetermined sense
Of unknown modes of being; O'er my thoughts
There hung a darkness, call it solitude
Or blank desertion. No familiar shapes
Remained, no pleasant images of trees,
Of sea or sky, no colours of green fields;
But huge and mighty forms that do not live
Like living men, moved slowly through the mind
By day, and were a trouble to my dreams.

The mountain peak which seemed to rise up menacingly, and deliberately to pursue the boy, may it not be taken as an embodiment of the same fears which 'from the utmost ends of the earth' surrounded the young Traherne? 'How did I know but dangers might suddenly arise from the East, and invade me from the unknown regions beyond the seas?' Although in Traherne's words there is no such explicit reference to the grim shape 'with purpose of its own' yet, diffused and implicit in his brief account, there is this very same sense of 'otherness',

. . . a dim and undetermined sense
Of unknown modes of being;

In both passages the familiar scene undergoes a sudden transformation. Traherne speaks of 'a certain want and horror . . . beyond imagination' which fell upon him. He is terrified by the wideness of the place. It is as if a sudden extension of the horizon, physically and spiritually, has taken place. The boy who is Wordsworth is troubled by a darkness, a solitude, a 'blank desertion'. The familiar has crumbled away before these 'huge and mighty forms' which are other than human in their stature.

This experience of Traherne's, which yet taught him that he was 'concerned in all the world' and that in the remotest borders there existed the causes of peace and beauty, could be regarded as an isolated instance of what Evelyn Underhill in her authoritative study *Mysticism*[1] describes as 'the awakening of the transcendental consciousness'. The essential fact of Traherne's experience, as he records it, is the change from a world which is centred around his own personality into another and larger universe of being. The early ecstasies of his life

[1] E. Underhill, *Mysticism* (London, 1912).

had centred on himself; but now the sense of 'otherness' disturbs his world. This is precisely the state of being which Miss Underhill finds typical of the first stage of the five stages which to her constitute the mystical life: 'It is a disturbance of the equilibrium of the self, which results in the shifting of the field of consciousness from lower to higher levels, with a consequent removal of the centre of interest from the subject to an object now brought into view: the necessary beginning of any process of transcendence.'[1]

This awakening of the self is to a presence which is as yet vaguely and incoherently apprehended. There is a reality existing outside the self which is still 'dim and undetermined'. Traherne writes again of this state in his poem *Nature*:[2]

> Here I was seated to behold New Things
> In the August-Mansion of the Kings of Kings;
> And All was mine. *The Author yet not known,*
> *But that there must be one was plainly shewn.* (ll. 77–80)

He is aware, on recollection, of the nature of this experience, and, later in the *Third Century*, as advice to others on the same road he writes: 'Therefore of necessity they must at first believe that Felicity is a glorious though an unknown thing' (*Centuries*, III 56). The sudden sense of glory, the comfort of 'hope and expectation' is undeniable, a certain fact on which to build. It may be momentary only and then withdrawn; in St Augustine's words, 'I was swept up to Thee by Thy Beauty, and torn away from Thee by my own weight.'[3] Traherne begins now (he gives no dates nor does he write in any consistently chronological order of experience) to experience intense intimations of Felicity. How often or at what interval these took place it is impossible to say. 'This spectacle,' he writes, 'once seen, will never be forgotten. It is a great part of the beatific vision. A sight of Happiness is Happiness' (*Centuries*, III, 60). The experience is supremely satisfying; this is the first positive affirmation Traherne makes of this state; secondly, because it is perfect it must be divine in its nature: 'I . . . knew there was a Deity because I was satisfied' (*Centuries*, III, 59). Here at the very outset we have an illustration of the essentially empirical nature of Traherne's conclusions. The reality of God is a fact of experience: that to Traherne is the base of all his subsequent reflections. In other words the unknown presence which has filled Traherne with both fear and yet a sudden exaltation,

---

[1] E. Underhill, *Mysticism* (London, 1912), p. 213.
[2] Op. cit., p. 65. My italics.   [3] Aug., *Conf.*, bk. VII, chap. XVII.

because of the positive and definite nature of his sensations, is given a similar positive and definite name; it is God, a real God, yet still not fully known. He exists as the undoubted source of a supremely satisfying experience to Traherne; 'This spectacle . . . is a great part of the beatific vision.' It is not the whole vision; that, if at all, is experienced at the final stage of the mystic's way. This is the first glimpse.

It will be clear that the theme which I am pursuing is that the stages through which the mystic passes are of first importance in arriving at any conclusion about the nature of Traherne's mysticism. That is their importance for the student; the point goes further still. The very quality of the experiences we are considering is affected by the means which have led to them. Both the final state and our appraisal of it are conditioned by the stages through which the mystic has passed. This is why I have maintained that, although Traherne at times states that he is rediscovering an experience already once known and enjoyed, and indeed though it may seem so to him, he is in effect proceeding to a new and original realization, that of a divine reality which is both transcendent and immanent. This realization must be present for the final experience to be consummated. It is evident that this realization is not present in Traherne's account of his childhood delight; nor is it yet fully to be discerned in what we have noted of these events in his spiritual history.

The time is due for a statement of the stages which have been distinguished as characteristic of some of the forms of Christian mystical life. I use here the classification arrived at by Evelyn Underhill.[1] Five stages are to be distinguished, although it should not be thought that they are distinct from each other or indeed inevitable. The divisions are diagrammatic, conveniences for a better understanding. The first stage is that of the sudden awakening of the individual to a reality existing outside himself, a reality felt to be divine: 'This experience, usually abrupt and well-marked, is accompanied by intense feelings of joy and exaltation.'[2] The experience is of an overwhelming sense of beauty in the world; in the case of Traherne it is not only a sense of beauty in the world of nature but in the very existence of people and things that overwhelmed him. His experience is momentary and occasional, but 'This spectacle once seen, will never be forgotten' (*Centuries*, III, 60). These passages from the *Third Century* might be taken as instances of the kind of experience which belongs to this first stage; but they do not offer any satisfactory evidence of the more sustained states of being

---

[1] E. Underhill, op. cit., pp. 205-7.　　　　[2] Op. cit., p. 205.

which would justify us in thinking that Traherne could be placed with the great contemplatives from whose experiences this classification is derived.

The second stage is that of purification. This is the attempt deliberately entered upon to remove the obstacles whatever they are which lie between the individual self and the reality he has momentarily apprehended:

> The Self, aware for the first time of Divine Beauty, realizes by contrast its own finiteness and imperfection, the manifold illusions in which it is immersed, the immense distance which separates it from the One. Its attempts to eliminate by discipline and mortification all that stands in the way of its progress towards union with God constitute Purgation: a state of pain and effort.[1]

The third stage is that of illumination, the contemplative state at its most effective point. It is the state of the full awareness of Divine Presence.

> When by Purgation the Self has become detached from the things of sense . . . its joyful consciousness of the Transcendent Order returns in an enhanced form. Like the prisoners in Plato's 'Cave of Illusion' it has awakened to knowledge of Reality, has struggled up the harsh and difficult path to the mouth of the cave. Now it looks upon the sun. This is Illumination.[2]

The fact concerning this state which must be emphasized is that it is the contemplation of divine reality; it is not the state of union. The individual contemplative retains still a sense of his own individuality. It is a state of intense happiness in which a relation exists between absolute reality as an object of awareness and the individual self as subject. Plotinus' image of the choric dancers moving about their divine master in the rhythm 'whereto the worlds keep time'[3] is quoted by Miss Underhill as of the essence of illumination. The supreme union has not yet been achieved but there is a 'willing and harmonious revolution about Him, that "in dancing we may know what is done". This distinction (i.e. between the dancer and that about which he is moving) holds good in almost every first-hand description of illumination which we possess: and it is this which marks it off from mystic union.'[4] The state of illumination 'forms, with the two preceding states the "first mystic life". Many mystics never go beyond it; and, on the other hand, many

---

[1] E. Underhill, op. cit., p. 205.   [2] Ibid., p. 206.
[3] Plotinus, *Ennead*, VI, 9.   [4] E. Underhill, op. cit., p. 282.

seers and artists not usually classed amongst them, have tasted, to some extent, the splendours of the illuminated state.'[1]

There remain two further stages; the fourth which is that of the last and complete purification of the self which ends in its annihilation. This is the stage of intense spiritual suffering which St John of the Cross called the dark night of the soul. The sense of exaltation which results from the perception of the presence of God, pervading all the objects of the mystic's contemplation, which marks the stage of illumination is changed now into an equally intense agony at the sense of God's absence. The withdrawal of His presence, once having been known, is all the more fearful. This stage is the final process of purification because in it the mystic learns to

> dissociate the personal satisfaction of mystical vision from the reality of mystical life. As in Purgation the senses were cleansed and humbled, and the energies and interests of the Self were concentrated upon transcendental things: so now the purifying process is extended to the very centre of I-hood, the will. The human instinct for personal happiness must be killed. This is the spiritual crucifixion so often described by the mystics: the great desolation in which the soul seems abandoned by the Divine. The Self now surrenders itself, its individuality, and its will, completely. It desires nothing, asks nothing, is utterly passive. . . .[2]

This last trial of the mystical experience prepares the way for the fifth and last state. This is the final end of the mystical life. 'In this state the Absolute Life is not merely perceived and enjoyed by the Self, as in Illumination: but is *one* with it. . . . It is a state of equilibrium, of purely spiritual life; characterized by peaceful joy, by enhanced powers, by intense certitude.'[3] This state of union is not to be identified with ecstasy. This is a sudden and temporary condition; brief and immediate enjoyments 'often experienced by the mystic in Illumination, or even on his first conversion. They cannot therefore be regarded as exclusively characteristic of the Unitive Way. In some, indeed—St Teresa is an example—the ecstatic trance seems to diminish rather than increase in frequency after the state of union has been attained.'[4] I note this as a point of some importance. In all the many instances that Miss Underhill collects of this final stage of union with divine reality it is the quality of enduring peace and utter certitude which is predominant. Furthermore, in the traditions of Christian mysticism this stage is marked also by a devotion to actual works in human society: 'You may think, my daughters, that the soul in this state should be so absorbed that she can

---

[1] Ibid., p. 206.   [2] Ibid., p. 206.   [3] Ibid., p. 207.   [4] Ibid., p. 207.

occupy herself with nothing. You deceive yourselves. She turns with greater ease and ardour than before to all which belongs to the service of God, and when these occupations leave her free again, she remains in the enjoyment of that companionship.'[1] It is as if in this ultimate life the mystic lives with God and man at the same time. He may have left the world in order to achieve this final consummation but having done so he resumes more fully than before his contact with the world. The mystic who has known the unitive life becomes a means whereby the power that works through him can be effectively released into human society:

> To go up alone into the mountain and come back as an Ambassador to the world, has ever been the method of humanity's best friends. This systole-and-diastole motion of retreat as the preliminary to a return remains the true ideal of Christian Mysticism in its highest development. Those in whom it is not found, however great in other respects they may be, must be considered as having stopped short of the final stage.[2]

These are the five stages characteristic of the history of many of the greatest figures in Christian mysticism.[3] In what relation does Traherne stand to this classification? Or is it relevant at all to what he writes? The broad answer is that while Traherne did enjoy the mystical experience of illumination and could express finely his sense of unity with creatures and things in this stage one cannot go further. In particular it is not possible to say that he knew anything of the difficulties of purgation or the desolation of the dark night of the soul. Traherne cannot be put with the great mystics. He is a visionary, an exponent of meditation, not a contemplative.

I have already noted the passage which could be brought to show his awakening to a new and more active consciousness of being:

> This taught me that I was concerned in all the world: and that in the remotest borders the causes of peace delight me, and the beauties of the earth when seen were made to entertain me: that I was made to hold a communion with the secrets of Divine Providence in all the world . . . the clear assurance of treasures everywhere, God's care and love, His goodness, wisdom, and power, His presence and watchfulness in all the ends of the earth, were my

---

[1] St Teresa, *El Castillo Interior*, Moradas Setimas, translated by the Benedictines of Stanbrook Abbey (London, 1906), chap. 1.

[2] E. Underhill, op. cit., p. 211.

[3] In arriving at these classifications Miss Underhill quotes extensively from St John of the Cross, St Teresa, St Catherine of Genoa, Eckhart, Suso, Tauler, St Francis of Assisi, George Fox and many others.

strength and assurance for ever: and that these things being absent to my eye, were my joys and consolations, as present to my understanding as the wideness and emptiness of the Universe which I saw before me (*Centuries*, III, 23).

This cannot, however, be said to represent any kind of a stage. It records an event only.

The second stage is that of purification. This is the conscious effort to know in more precise and positive shape the hidden and mysterious presence of which he has become suddenly aware. It is the process of cleansing the gates of the senses so that these joys and consolations of which he here writes shall be as present to his eye as they were to his understanding: 'The beauties of the earth when seen were made to entertain me', 'Everything in its place is admirable, deep and glorious: out of its place like a wandering bird, is desolate and good for nothing. How therefore it relateth to God and all creatures must be seen before it can be enjoyed' (*Centuries*, III, 55). For these things to be seen purification is necessary. The observer is at fault.[1] Traherne constantly insists on this. The normal man in human society sees the world of men and things for the most part in terms of his own interests; he imposes a pattern which reflects himself upon the external world. He does not in fact see the world as it is. Traherne writes of the need therefore for self-amendment: 'All things were well in their proper places, I alone was out of frame and had need to be mended' (*Centuries*, III, 60). The world of 'outward things', Traherne insists, does not need alteration or improvement; 'They lay so well, methought, they would not be mended: but I must be mended to enjoy them' (*Centuries*, III, 60). It is the self, the so called individual self which is the obstacle to the enjoyment of this deep and glorious world, the enjoyment which is Felicity.[2] Evil is not an objective reality; it is for him rather a characteristic of the mind, almost indeed simply a matter of bad habits. The self that has been built by education, convention and habit, the self that is the product of environment and routine must be purified:

> For we must disrobe ourselves of all false colours, and unclothe our souls of evil habits; all our thoughts must be infant-like and clear; the powers of

---

[1] Tis not the Object, but the Light,
   That maketh Hev'n: 'Tis a clearer Sight,
     Felicity
Appears to none but them that purely see.
         (*The Preparative*, ll. 57–60)

[2] 'All other things are well; I only, and the sons of men about me, are disordered' (*Centuries*, III, 30).

our soul free from the leaven of this world, and disentangle from men's conceits and customs. Grit in the eye or yellow jaundice will not let a man see those objects truly that are before it. And therefore it is requisite that we should be as very strangers to the thoughts, customs, and opinions of men in this world, as if we were but little children (*Centuries*, III, 5).

Traherne shows himself here as aware of the necessity for purification without revealing however that he himself is involved in any such process. He writes as a preceptor only, of what is, in any case, stock Christian doctrine.

Two processes are implied in what Traherne has written in these examples; the first is that of the amendment of the self, the second that of the removal of the obstacles which obscure the perception of divine order. The two processes are not distinct from each other; for instance the sense of self, of being an individual and separate existence, may be one of the most obstinate of distractions. Furthermore the whole endeavour of purification is not begun by the exercise of a cool, well-balanced knowledge of the need for new adjustment. This knowledge is present indeed but it is enveloped in the urgent and, as Traherne has written, instinctive desire for the Felicity he has momentarily seen. In other words the whole activity of his life is to be orientated to this transcendent end. His aim is this—and Traherne speaks, as he usually does, in generalizations—to achieve the state of one who

> having proposed to himself a superior end than is commonly supposed, bears all discouragements, breaks through all difficulties and lives unto it: that having seen the secrets and the secret beauties of the highest reason, orders his conversation, and lives by rule: though in this age it be held never so strange that he should do so. Only he is Divine because he does this upon noble principles, because God is, because Heaven is, because Jesus Christ hath redeemed him, and because he loves Him; not only because virtue is amiable and felicity is delightful, but for that also (*Centuries*, IV, 8).

The lesser is to be included in the greatest. Virtue is amiable but that is not the reason for pursuing it; Felicity may be delightful but only because of the existence of the absolute principle 'because God is, because Heaven is, because Jesus Christ hath redeemed him, and because he loves Him'.

Traherne says nothing of the details of the method by which the amendment of the self is to be brought about. He states the principles however quite unequivocally. The order he gives is significant: 'Love God, Angels and Men, triumph in God's works, delights in God's laws, take pleasure in God's ways in all ages, correct sins, bring good out of evil, subdue your lusts, order your senses, conquer the customs and opinions of men and render good for evil' (*Centuries*, IV, 38). In other words the love of God is not only the cause of his entrance in this 'true government of our passions' by which 'we disentangle them from impediments, and fit and guide them to their proper objects' (*Centuries*, II, 100). It is the very means by which this true government may be achieved. To Traherne it is love which is the most effective means of achieving the Felicity he seeks; it is the very desire for purification, for self-amendment that is stressed in his words here as instrumental in the realization of this end.

The love of Felicity must be combined with an intellectual conviction, the conviction that all things are directly concerned with the enjoyment of Felicity. We must believe this, Traherne says, as an essential preliminary to the experience of this enjoyment: 'All things are ours; all things serve us and minister to us, could we find the way: nay they are all ours, and serve us so perfectly, that they are best enjoyed in their proper places: even from the sun to a sand, from a cherubim to a worm . . .' (*Centuries*, IV, 16). We must believe that God is good before we know His goodness. That direct knowledge comes with the third stage, that of illumination. By what discipline we are to believe this Traherne does not say. We do not read in Traherne of the suffering and mortification that marks the history of other Christian mystics in the effort of purification. For instance, he speaks of the loneliness of the way: 'One great discouragement to Felicity, or rather to great souls in the pursuit of Felicity, is the solitariness of the way that leadeth to her temple. A man that studies happiness must sit *alone like a sparrow upon the house-top, and like a pelican in the wilderness*' (*Centuries*, IV, 13). Traherne was thinking here of Psalm 102. The half line that comes between these two references is omitted. (Traherne is quoting from memory: he reverses the order; in the Psalm, 'I am like a pelican of the wilderness' comes before 'as a sparrow alone upon the house-top'). The missing half line is 'I am like an owl of the desert'. The omission is significant. Traherne leaves out the desert and complains of the solitariness of the way. He would prefer company. This is not the attitude of the mystic who deliberately chooses to experience the spiritual privations which the desert symbolizes. We are not aware in Traherne's prose of the profound effort and suffering which mystical purification will involve. There is an almost perfunctory tone in his advice to become again as little children as if nothing could be easier or more simple: 'And therefore it is requisite that we should be as very strangers to the thoughts, customs, and opinions of men in this world, as if we were but little children' (*Centuries*, III, 5). Traherne does not express anywhere the experience of purgation, the surrender of the self. What we do find is orthodox exhortation to self-control, disciplining of the will and the recapture of simplicity and naturalness. But we are not presented with any concretely realized image of these processes.

Traherne regards the nature of man as capable of Felicity provided that the distorting film of education, opinion, custom and prejudice is purged away. The mind and the senses, once amended, once 'in frame', can see God. Traherne does not refer to the necessity of grace for the Felicity of the divine vision to be enjoyed; furthermore original sin does not enter into Traherne's scheme except as accounting for a tendency to fall into error, to value the wrong things. We are impelled to enquire into Traherne's assumption of the goodness of man's nature. Incidentally this enquiry will also illuminate the lack of emphasis which Traherne places on the process of purification. Traherne places on a level of equivalence Adam before the fall, the direct and unsullied vision of the child and the amended man, who, having put himself 'in frame', is capable of the vision of God in the world. Furthermore he asserts that the human senses are means of knowledge that are to be trusted,

> For simple Sense
> Is Lord of all created Excellence.

The disabilities which resulted from the fall of man, the depravity which original sin has stamped on the human form do not appear as gross impurities in Traherne's world because for him they have ceased to exist. The excellence of human nature represented by Adam before the Fall has been restored; man has been redeemed, is redeemed indeed, by Christ, and therefore original sin no longer infects humanity. Traherne's belief in the purity and goodness of his perceptions seems often to involve a belief in the 'natural' goodness of man. He believes in original innocence more than in original sin. It is rather that Traherne, believing completely that Christ has redeemed mankind, asserts that man can once more become a true image of God. The solution seems easy for him. All that is necessary for the divine original to be known is for the 'dirty devices' of the world to be cleansed away. Man can know God; can resume a divinity by union with God 'because God is, because Heaven is, *because Jesus Christ hath redeemed him,*[1] and because

[1] My italics.

he loves Him' (*Centuries*, IV, 8). The goodness of human nature is a present fact to Traherne because of the historical Redemption and its ever present effects. The battle has been won for man did he but know it, and no further effort is necessary. This is the reason, I suggest, why we find in Traherne nothing of the intense labour of purification and the dying to self of which record is to be found in the history of other mystics. Apart from an isolated phrase, 'the abyss of humility' (*Centuries*, III, 48), there is no indication that Traherne had ever known the inner conflicts which precede the 'self surrender which is the mainspring of the mystic life'.[1]

There is, however, a brief passage in the *Centuries* in which Traherne refers to a process of major importance for the achievement of Felicity. The sense of self is a formidable obstacle to the sense of union with God and therefore to get rid of it is a major problem. This is the solution which Traherne gives; he is speaking in the third person:

> He was a strict and severe applier of all things to himself, and would first have his self-love satisfied, and then his love of all others. It is true that self-love is dishonourable, but then it is when it is alone. And self-endedness is mercenary, but then it is when it endeth in oneself. It is more glorious to love others, and more desirable, but by natural means to be attained. That pool must first be filled that shall be made to overflow. He was ten years studying before he could satisfy his self-love. And now finds nothing more easy than to love others better than oneself. And that to love mankind so is the comprehensive method to all Felicity (*Centuries*, IV, 55).

This passage is important in several directions. It contains an interesting comment on what may be taken as the period of devotion before the individual self-hood of the man was put in its proper place of noble subservience to God. The love of self was transformed into the love of others after a period of 'ten years studying'. Further we have here a re-affirmation of Traherne's conviction that 'to love others better than oneself . . . is the comprehensive method to all Felicity'. Finally, it forms a link, as I shall show later, with traditional medieval doctrine of the relation between love of self and love of God.

'That pool must first be filled that shall be made to overflow.' The self-love, which is natural, must be the means by which the love of others, which in a sense is unnatural, is to be achieved. In other words it must not be suppressed or forced to comply with a discipline imposed by the will. It must first be fulfilled; self-love must be satisfied,

---

[1] E. Underhill, op. cit., p. 269.

not denied. We must want to love others, not feel that we ought to do so, and this desire to love will not be forced; it will come only as a development of a positive activity. Traherne's assertion is that love creates love. Love for others cannot spring from hatred of the self. Traherne's comment is a profound truth. The self must be amended but not despised; the realization of the dignity and the value of others depends first on the realization of one's own nature, and of one's own due claims.

The condition that Traherne makes, and it is one of critical importance, is that this love for the self which is natural and right,[1] if it is to be the point of departure for the greater experience of Felicity, must not remain exclusively centred on the self: 'Self-endedness is mercenary . . . when it ended in oneself. It is more glorious to love others, and more desirable, but by natural means to be attained' (*Centuries*, IV, 55). The self is to be purified through the self; the transference from a universe centred on the self to a universe having a different object as its centre and which includes the self as a necessary component is to be made by means which the self approves. The implications of Traherne's thought here is that we cannot truly love others and presumably we cannot love God simply by denying ourselves. The self is not to be by-passed; otherwise our so-called love for others will simply be a form of self-love. We will love God in the image of ourselves. The just claims of the individual and personal man must first be met before a real orientation towards God is possible:

> Had we not loved ourselves at all, we could never have been obliged to love anything. So that self-love is the basis of all love. But when we do love ourselves, and self-love is satisfied infinitely in all its desires and possible demands, then it is easily led to regard the Benefactor more than itself, and for his sake overflows abundantly to all others (*Centuries*, IV, 55).[2]

What we do not know is precisely by what means, by what studies, self-love is satisfied, 'in all its desires and possible demands'. These details Traherne does not tell us, and by omitting them Traherne gives to his statements a certain deceptive and general quality which has the effect of minimizing the difficulties of this development.[3] The 'ten years

[1] 'Not to love oneself at all is brutish, or rather absurd and stonish, (for the beasts do love themselves)' (*Centuries*, IV, 55).

[2] The resemblance of this doctrine to St Bernard's *De Diligendo Deo* is discussed in chapters VI and VIII.

[3] The classic example of a deceptively easy injunction is St Augustine's 'Love, and do as you will'; 'Dilige et quod vis fac' (*In Joann.*, vii, 8).

studying', for instance, is mentioned only in a casual phrase. Again, like the use of the third person, I take this as a sign of the diminishing importance to Traherne of his own individuality. In the process of satisfying self-love he is becoming less and less self-centred. The more he turns towards God the less important seem to him the details of his own private experience. The more general and impersonal therefore his statements become. Yet he is aware of what is happening and that there is a contrast between what can be stated easily and simply and what can be attained only with difficulty. It is a step towards detachment from the self, towards the placing 'in frame' of the personal being we normally are. It is so in this sense. Consider this passage:

> A man should know the blessings he enjoyeth: A man should prize the blessings which he knoweth: A man should be thankful for the benefits which he prizeth: A man should rejoice in that for which he is thankful. These are easy things, and so are those also which are drowned in a deluge of errors and customs;[1] That blessings the more they are, are the sweeter; the more they serve, if lovers and friends, the more delightful, yet these are the hard lessons, in a perverse and retrograde world, to be practised: and almost the only lesson necessary to its enjoyment (*Centuries*, IV, 54).

These necessary lessons are 'easy things'. Traherne is aware of the requisite means towards Felicity. He is sure of their formulation. It is easy therefore to state them verbally in a form which is simple and clear. It is in this sense that these things are easy, 'very easy, and infinitely noble; very noble, and productive of unspeakable good'. Elsewhere Traherne writes: 'Nothing is so easy as to yield one's assent to glorious principles' (*Centuries*, IV, 52). I find the very form in which Traherne has expressed these 'glorious principles' remarkable. He writes them as a formula, with the repetitions of an incantation. 'Blessings', 'prize', 'thankful', the words are repeated with liturgical ceremony. Then in complete contrast, with strict matter of factness, these easy things are firmly stated to be hard lessons, obscure 'to find . . . difficult to practice' . . . 'in a perverse and retrograde world'. Traherne deliberately points the contrast between knowing what is to be done and the effective practice of that knowledge, between formal understanding and realization in terms of his complete being of such formal understanding. This passage is an indication of his knowledge that real rejoicing, real thankfulness does not come about by saying 'I rejoice' or 'I am thankful', however much we may mean these statements.

[1] Cf. 'the torrent of Use and Wont'. St Augustine, *Confessions*, bk. I, chap. 16.

Thankfulness and rejoicing in so far as they are means to Felicity are more than verbal utterances; they must be states of being, including and surpassing verbal formulation. This knowledge that Traherne reveals here is to be regarded as forming an element in the process of self-amendment in so far as it makes a distinction between the man who knows and the man who is, and implies that the two must be brought into harmony if Felicity is to be found. It is the advance in impersonal examination which is important; it is an advance in self-knowledge. I take this to be the real significance of this passage, a significance which goes deeper than, but does not dispense with, the surface meaning that it is easy to say what one should do and yet difficult to do it. The surface meaning has its own relevance in so far as it conveys a realistic attitude to what one might describe as the technical problems of the study of Felicity. The passage I have been considering comes close in its place in the *Fourth Century* to the remarkable section which insists on self-love as the basis for all love. There is a connection. As I shall point out in more detail in a later chapter Traherne conceives of love as a mode of knowledge. The satisfaction of self-love in Traherne's meaning includes, I think, the development of self-knowledge, of an objective attitude towards oneself which is necessary if the pool is to be filled in order that it shall overflow.

I have said that Traherne does not tell us in detail in what ways self-love is to be satisfied and that this very omission is significant. This statement should be qualified. The filling of the pool which is necessary for the overflowing to others of the love which is the comprehensive means to Felicity is closely linked with Traherne's attitude towards the bodily senses. This is an important subject in a study of Traherne and deserves separate discussion. I mention it now because the satisfying of self-love by respecting 'Its desires and possible demands' is to be seen as a necessary part of this attitude. The senses are to be fully exercised because God can be known by them:

> My Palat is a Touch-stone fit
> To taste how Good Thou Art.[1]
> (*The Estate*, ll. 15–16)

Our self-love is to be satisfied by

> A due Emploiment of our Faculties.

---

[1] Op. cit., p. 81.

This is good, Traherne holds, because it is a mode of praising God. The body is part of God's creation and

> Each Toe, each Finger, by thy powerful Skill
>   Created, should distil
> Ambrosia; more than Nectar flow
>   From evry Joint I ow,
> B'ing well-imploy'd; for they Thy Holy Will
> Are activ Instruments made to fulfill.[1]
>
> (ll. 23–8)

This is a substantial ground for the ten years studying to satisfy self-love; to study the ways in which the Holy Will is to be fulfilled by these active instruments, the bodily senses, the great endowments of hand and eye, with all their 'desires and possible demands'. Paradoxically as it might seem, the senses are to be purified by their proper employment; the self is to be amended by realizing its true nature, and discarding 'vain affections'. The objects of sensory experience must be realized without interference from the 'meddling intellect'. Metaphor, for instance, must be discarded. The naked truth is to be known only by the naked being, stripped of all conscious and 'contrived' encumbrances. The true excellence of the world is only seen

> When we all *Metaphors* remov;
> For, Metaphors conceal,
> And only Vapors prov.[2]
> (*The Person*, ll. 24–5)

The end of the process of self-amendment is to clear away the metaphors so that the bodily senses can receive

> The tru Ideas of all Things
> (*The Preparative*, l. 25)

The individual must put himself into a 'wise passiveness', surrender himself to the influence of the natural creation, if he is to realize God in the world.

> Let Verity
> Be thy Delight: Let me esteem
> True Wealth far more than Toys:
> Let Sacred Riches be,
> While the fictitious only seems,

---

[1] Ibid.   [2] Op. cit., p. 77.

My Reall Joys:
For Golden Chains and Bracelets are
But gilded Manacles, whereby
Old *Satan* doth ensnare,
Allure, bewitch the Eye.
The Gifts, O God, alone I'll prize
My Tongue, my Eys,
My Cheeks, my Lips, mine Ears, my Hands, my Feet
Their Harmony is far more sweet,
Their Beauty tru. And these, in all my Ways,
Shall be the Themes and Organs of thy Prais.[1]
(*The Person*, ll. 49–64)

Traherne's search for 'Reall Joys', his discarding of the fictitious, his trust in the senses to reveal the truth unimpeded by words or metaphors, his belief in the harmony of the natural order to be perceived by the child-like mind are not in themselves signs of mystical experience. All these things could be described as part of the characteristic movement of his times, the movement heralded by Francis Bacon. Bacon for instance speaks of the necessity to submit the mind to 'things'; he advocates a spirit of humility: 'Nor could we hope to succeed, if we arrogantly searched for the sciences in the narrow cells of the human understanding and not submissively in the wider world',[2] and, as Professor Willey points out, entrance to the kingdom of man which is based on the sciences is similar to the entrance 'to the kingdom of heaven, where no admission is conceded except to children'.[3]

Wherein lies the difference? Is Bacon a mystic? or is Traherne a typical seventeenth-century thinker who is simply using a set of terms which mask his real destination which is in the bosom of John Locke? The difference lies in this. Bacon distrusts the 'meddling intellect' because it obscures the observation and the explanation of the natural world. His purification is a matter of scientific method, for him the most effective method; the mind must be free from preconceptions about the nature of things, in particular those of scholastic theology. The submission of the whole self to things, which he advocates, is in order that these things shall be known objectively. Traherne's object is not the study of things for their own sake but for God's sake. His objection to words and metaphors is that they interfere with the enjoyment of God and his creation. To Traherne there is only one truth,

[1] Op. cit., p. 79.   [2] Bacon, *De Augmentis*, Bohn ed., p. 10.
[3] Bacon, *Nov. Org.*, ed. Fowler, LXVIII, p. 256.

'that God is', and the end of human activity is to know that truth, and, finally, to enjoy the perfection of its presence. God is not simply in nature to be enjoyed by the senses. He is also infinite and absolute. A sense of mystery is always with Traherne, the mystery of a Being who is both immanent and transcendent. This does not mean that a claim is therefore put forward for seeing Traherne as a mystic in his devotion to 'the tru Ideas of all Things', certainly not in the terms of the five stages. His amendment cannot be called mystical purgation but rather the attempt to recapture the singleness and purity of vision of the child with its whole-hearted wonder at the very existence of things. That he does indeed achieve this vision is his distinctive quality.

CHAPTER IV

The Illumination of Traherne

THE third stage of the mystical life is that which is described as Illumination which, again to quote Evelyn Underhill, is the realization by the purified self 'of a world that was always there, and wherein its substantial being—that Ground which is of God—has always stood'.[1] This is the mystical experience which Traherne most clearly shows.

The mystic apprehends God both as immanent and transcendent. These two terms demand comment; I will take the second first. The mystical apprehension of God as transcendent emphasizes the absolute difference existing between the world of sense perception and the Absolute Godhead. This ultimate source is utterly remote, a hidden God which yet underlies the world of phenomena. It is unknowable by the senses or the reason of men. The mysticism of the pseudo-Dionysius and the fourteenth-century English mystics of the same tradition is of this nature. A separation is implied between the human and the divine, between the temporal and the eternal worlds. The mystic who apprehends reality with this emphasis on the transcendence of the Godhead uses characteristically the language of exile; he thinks of life as a difficult pilgrimage, and of God as a remote and unknown power. Henry Vaughan, for instance, illustrated in some respects this attitude. In the poem *Man* he writes:

> He knows he hath a home, but scarce knows where:
> He says it is so far
> That he hath quite forgot how to get there.
> He knocks at all doors, strays and roams.[2]

He is acutely aware of the distance which separates him from the perfection he has glimpsed, and is sensitive to his own imperfection, here in this life, where

> My days, which are at best but dull and hoary,
> Mere glimmering and decays,[3]

---

[1] E. Underhill, op. cit., p. 280.
[2] *The Works of Henry Vaughan*, ed. Martin (Oxford, 1914), vol. II, p. 477.
[3] Ibid., p. 484.

fill him with a sense of loss. This is the state which William James has called that of the 'sick soul'.[1]

The other extreme is the apprehension of God as immanent. This implies a belief that the search for the Absolute does not involve a long and difficult journey but lies in the realization of that which is already implicit in the self and in the universe. God is not wholly external to anyone, but 'is present with all things, though they are ignorant that He is so'.[2] God does not hold aloof from an imperfect world but dwells within the shifting phenomena of the temporal universe. He is at hand to be discovered by those who have eyes and ears to see and hear. The treasures of the immanent God are 'immediately near to the very gates of our senses' (*Centuries*, I, 23). All that is necessary for their enjoyment is purity. In the words of Eckhart, 'God is nearer to me than I am to myself; He is just as near to wood and stone, but they do not know it.'[3] Those who seek God in this way do not, like Henry Vaughan, 'long to travel back' to a home not to be found in the so-called normal world. They look within themselves and find

> A secret Self . . . enclos'd within,
> That was not bounded with my Cloaths or Skin.

These are Traherne's words from his poem *Nature*.[4] This secret self underlying the self which is the product of environment, education and the pressures of opinion and convention can make immediate contact with God. In the inner recesses of his being the mystic realizes the divine principle which is latent both in the universe and in man. The world of nature enshrines the absolute God; it is not a projection of it: 'I understood', says St Teresa, 'how our Lord was in all things, and how He was in the soul.'[5] The theory of immanence unless controlled by a dogmatic structure can pass easily into pantheism and into 'extravagant perversions of the doctrine of deification in which the mystic holds his transfigured self to be identical with the Indwelling God'.[6]

These are the contexts to be held in mind when the terms transcendent and immanent are used in this discussion. The inclination of Traherne towards the immanent God is obvious. Unlike Vaughan,

---

[1] W. James, *Varieties of Religious Experience* (Cambridge, Mass., 1925), Lecture VI.

[2] Plotinus, *Ennead*, VI, 9.

[3] Eckhart (1260–1329), *Predigten*, trans. C. Field (London, 1909), LXIX.

[4] Op. cit., p. 61.   [5] St Teresa, *Relaccion* (Lewis' trans.), ix, 10.

[6] E. Underhill, op. cit., p. 119.

Traherne is at home in the visible world. Yet his writings record also the acknowledgement if not the experience of the transcendent God. It is his essential quality to seek the infinite and imageless Godhead through the world of finite and sensible forms. Both modes of apprehension are present in the characteristic expressions of Traherne's mystical experience. For instance the deity indicated in these words is the transcendent Godhead: 'The infinity of God is infinitely profitable as well as great; as glorious as incomprehensible: so far from straightening that it magnifieth all things. And must be seen in you, or God will be absent: Nothing less than infinite is God, and *as finite He cannot be enjoyed*'[1] (*Centuries*, IV, 73). This could be taken to point to the incomprehensible, remote and impersonal God. On the other hand, here is the immanent God revealed in words remarkably similar to those of Eckhart which I have already quoted: 'The truth of it is it (*sc.* infinity) is individually in the soul: for God is there and more near to us than we are to ourselves' (*Centuries*, II, 81). At the moment I wish to do no more than place these two highly significant passages side by side as evidence of Traherne's mystical vision of God as both transcendent and immanent. With this firmly in mind let us consider what is the characteristic nature of Traherne's experience, the apprehension of divine reality clearly and demonstrably in the physical world.

The process of purification for Traherne has been simply 'to unlearn . . . the dirty devices of this world' (*Centuries*, III, 3). By the means of the highest reason, above all by love, turning from the self towards men and through them to God, Traherne comes to the joyful apprehension of absolute reality:

> His soul recovered its pristine liberty, and saw through the mud wall of flesh and blood. Being alive, he was in the spirit all his days. While his body therefore was inclosed in this world, his soul was in the temple of Eternity, and clearly beheld the infinite life and omnipresence of God: having conversation with invisible, spiritual, and immaterial things, which were its companions, itself being invisible, spiritual and immaterial. Kingdoms and Ages did surround him as clearly as the hills and mountains: and therefore the kingdom of God was ever round about him. Everything was one way or other his sovereign delight and transcendent pleasure, as in Heaven everything will be everyone's peculiar treasure (*Centuries*, III, 95).

This is the experience of illumination. Traherne sees the world in a dual aspect; things in time are interpenetrated with a sense of their

---

[1] My italics.

timelessness. He realizes that his life is lived simultaneously on the planes of time and eternity. The sense of divine presence goes side by side with the daily life of the man: 'He saw God face to face in this earthly Tabernacle' (*Centuries*, III, 94). Living in the body and living the life of the body, at the same time he converses with 'invisible, spiritual, and immaterial things'.

What is particularly to be noted here is that Traherne is still aware of himself as a separate entity. He is in a state of contemplation in which he 'converses' with the divine reality. It is a communion with God; it is not the supreme mystical experience of union with God. Furthermore Traherne retains a sense of other distinctions. Not only is he aware of himself as conversing with some Other not himself; he is also aware of himself as a conscious thinking being. For instance, he writes of his vision of 'the Kingdom of God . . . ever round about him' in the world of men and things as that which was realized 'only in the light of faith . . . and yet', he goes on to say, he 'rejoiced as if he had seen them by the Light of Heaven' (*Centuries*, III, 96). In other words he makes a deliberate distinction between the light of faith and the light of Heaven. Yet both lights are able to reveal a comparable splendour. These points are noteworthy. First, there is Traherne's awareness of a subject-object relationship, between himself and a world of 'invisible, spiritual and immaterial things'. This is implied in his use of the word 'converse'; second, there is the indication of the relation between what in mystical phraseology is the stage of illumination and the stage of the unitive life. Traherne illustrates this first distinction in several short passages grouped closely together in the middle sections of the *Third Century*. I take them as typical instances of what Evelyn Underhill considers as distinctively characteristic of this stage of illumination: 'The real distinction between the Illumination and the Unitive Life is that in Illumination the individuality of the subject—however profound his spiritual consciousness, however close his communion with the Infinite—remains separate and intact.'[1]

In the 65th Meditation of the *Third Century* Traherne is engaged in a reflection on the nature of God, thinking in the terms of scholasticism. He has been previously speaking in Thomist phrases of God as the complete actualization of the potential. God is complete and single, not a composite being.[2] This leads Traherne to the impassioned contemplation of the perfection of God and the realization that 'all things were contained in Him from all Eternity' (*Centuries*, III, 65). The

[1] E. Underhill, op. cit., p. 295.   [2] *Centuries*, III, 64.

scholastic phrases become quickened with a sense of expectancy; the logic unfolds the reality and conviction is transformed into realization. The operations of the intellect are alive with the sense of God as an immediate and actual presence: 'All things being now to be seen and contemplated in His bosom; and advanced therefore into a Divine Light, being infinitely older and more precious than we were aware. Time itself being in God eternally' (*Centuries*, III, 65). This is the sudden point of illumination; the complete understanding, an understanding which may not be permanent, of the nature of the timeless God. On reflection Traherne acknowledges this apex of experience: 'Little did I imagine that, while I was thinking these things I was conversing with God' (*Centuries*, III, 66). The experience is, for Traherne, personal and immediate. His state of heightened consciousness appears to him unique: 'I was so ignorant that I did not think any man in the World had had such thoughts before' (*Centuries*, III, 66). Yet he had been quoting from the 38th *Oration* of St Gregory Nazienzen immediately before. His ignorance lay not so much in lack of information as in incomplete belief in his information. It is when he fully believes what he knows that a re-orientation of his whole consciousness takes place.

What is to be discerned in these passages is the personal satisfaction of mystical vision. A new world has opened out. The individual self sees all things with new eyes; he rejoices in the discovery of divine reality:

> Upon this I began to believe that all other creatures were such that God was Himself in their creation, that is Almighty Power wholly exerted; and that every creature is indeed as it seemed in my infancy, not as it is commonly apprehended. Everything being sublimely rich and great and glorious. Every spire of every grass is the work of His hand: And I in a world where everything is mine, and far better than the greater sort of children esteem diamonds and pearls to be. Gold and silver being the very refuse of nature, and the worst things in God's Kingdom: Howbeit being truly good in their proper places (*Centuries*, III, 62).

Traherne has attained a new level of consciousness; in a strangely matter of fact phrase, he is 'satisfied in God' (*Centuries*, III, 63). He has achieved the purity and simplicity of vision which the person of the child symbolizes. It is to be remarked that he writes now that the splendour of creation is real to his illuminated sight whereas the childhood excellencies are now described as 'seeming', an appearance only. In all this the sense of personal discovery is intense; he is still himself, an amended, purified self certainly, but still himself. In these conversings, in this beholding face to face his sense of individuality remains separate and intact. There is no indication of the complete surrender of the self which separates the personal satisfaction of mystical vision from the reality of mystical life.

An essential quality of this new vision which Traherne now enjoys lies in an increased sensitivity to the phenomenal world. This enlargement of consciousness is in itself a source of pleasure superior to any which the ordinary level of consciousness can provide. Yet this enhanced vision is not itself final. The world of phenomena is seen always against a larger background. Traherne speaks of the new light that darts into the world, as a means of discovering a further reality: 'God by this means bringing me into the very heart of His Kingdom' (*Centuries*, III, 66). A little later he writes:

> I evidently saw that the way to become rich and blessed was not by heaping accidental and devised riches to make ourselves great in the vulgar manner, but to approach more nearer, or to see more clearly with the eye of our understanding, the beauties and glories of the whole world: *and to have communion with the Deity in the riches of God and Nature*[1] (*Centuries*, III, 67).

The last words of this passage provide an example to indicate that Traherne's vision was of a different order from that simply of a seventeenth-century divine, pious, devout and charitable and gifted with a talent for writing in prose.

George Herbert in *The Pulley* distinguishes God from the nature He has created:

> For if I should (said He)
> Bestow this jewel[2] also on my creature,
> He would adore my gifts instead of Me,
> And rest in Nature, not the God of Nature:
> So both should losers be.[3]

The world of nature cannot provide man's final peace, nor is God to be identified with his gifts. Traherne goes even further. Not only is God distinguished from Nature, but a third term, the Deity, is introduced as anterior to both: 'to have communion with the Deity in the riches of God and Nature'. As Traherne has written it the Deity is the ultimate

[1] My italics.
[2] I.e. Rest.
[3] *The Works of George Herbert*, ed. F. E. Hutchison (Oxford, 1941), p. 160.

towards which the riches both of God and Nature may lead. Traherne here, I suggest, uses the term Deity to stand for the Godhead which is used in traditional mystical terminology, the Unconditioned Absolute. By Deity I take Traherne to mean the imageless, wordless, impersonal reality with which it is the mystic's final destination to become united. The terms God and Nature contain by contrast an element of anthropomorphism. Traherne is still an individual personality; his enjoyment even in his purified state of the riches of God and Nature involves in some degree a personal image. Like may only speak to like. Traherne converses with God. He is not yet united with the Deity which underlies both God and Nature. This union cannot take place while he remains the person he is. The final surrender of the self must first be made. Therefore God and Nature still retain for him in some degree a reflection of himself as a person; but he is aware that there is a further reality transcending the limitations of Nature, and of God as revealed or as conceived. This is the infinite and unconditioned Deity. Traherne hints at his awareness of this ultimate by his use of a third term which is distinct from both God and Nature; distinct but not alien because it is by means of the riches of Nature and of God that this ultimate reality is 'enjoyed'. This incomprehensible Godhead cannot be consciously known; it can only be experienced. The self which can experience the unspeakable joy of this union must cease to be a personality in the sense in which we normally use the term. Traherne's words, however, remain an isolated phrase only and although they may be taken as indicating an awareness of deity in this sense it would be unwarranted to put too much weight on them.

The examples I have considered so far indicate Traherne's apprehension of a divine reality to be discerned in the world round about him, his apprehension of divinity in a blade of grass: 'therefore the Kingdom of God was ever round about him' (*Centuries*, III, 95). The realization of God in this earthly Tabernacle is, however, by no means the only source of mystical illumination for Traherne. There is another and, I think, for him a more important experience which brings him into the 'marvellous Light' (*Centuries*, I, 99). (The imagery of Light, as Evelyn Underhill points out, is widely used by mystical writers in this stage of illumination. Traherne is no exception.)[1] This is the realization within him of a secret self, a self which is at the same

---

[1] T. S. Eliot writes of 'that imagery of *light* which is the form of certain types of mystical experience', *Selected Essays* (London, 1932), p. 267 (the essay on Dante).

time infinite and universal. The most remarkable expression of this
experience is to be found in the poem *My Spirit*:[1]

> My naked simple Life was I:
>   That Act so strongly shin'd
> Upon the Earth, the Sea, the Sky,
> It was the Substance of the Mind;
>   The Sense its self was I.
> I felt no Dross nor Matter in my Soul,
> No Brims nor Borders, such as in a Bowl
> We see: My Essence was *Capacity*.
>   *That* felt all things:
>   The Thought that springs
> There-from's its self: It hath no other Wings
>   To spread abroad, nor Eys to see,
>   Nor pair of Hands to feel,
>   Nor knees to kneel:
> But being Simple, like the Deity,
>   In its own Center is a Sphere,
>   Not limited, but evry-where.
>
> (ll. 1–17)

The essential experience of this poem seems to be Traherne's sense of
his unlimited power to become the very object of his contemplation.[2]
This is to be seen also in *The Preparative*:

> Then was my Soul my only All to me,
>   A living endless Ey,
>   Scarce bounded with the Sky,
> Whose power, and Act, and Essence was to see:
> I was an inward Sphere of Light,
> Or an interminable Orb of Sight,
>   Exceeding that which makes the Days,
> A *vital* Sun that shed abroad his Rays:
>   All Life, all Sense,
> A naked, simple, pure Intelligence.[3]
>
> (ll. 11–20)

---

[1] Op. cit., p. 51.

[2] This made me present evermore
With whatsoere' I saw.
Op. cit., p. 53.

[3] Op. cit., p. 21.

The objects of his perception are irradiated by the light which seems to come from within him, a light which is superior to that of the sun. The living spirit absorbs and surpasses the physical senses. As the distinction between body and spirit disappears so likewise is Traherne unable to distinguish between what is objective and what is subjective:

> And evry Object in my Heart, a Thought
> Begot or was: I could not tell
>   Whether the Things did there
>   Themselves appear,
>   Which in my *Spirit* truly seem'd to dwell:
>   Or whether my conforming Mind
>   Were not ev'n all that therein shin'd.[1]
>
> (*My Spirit*, ll. 45-51)

He creates and is created by the world around him, the world which seems to flow through him. The terms internal and external which are useful on ordinary levels of consciousness cease to be valid for him. The simplicity of this state of being, his 'naked, simple, pure intelligence', stands clearly for an absence of all dualism, a positive sense of unity in which the distinctions of spirit and sense, mind and body, subject and object become subordinate to an overriding conviction of an essentially mutual relationship existing between apparently individual and separate entities. Traherne gives great weight to the word simple. To be simple is to be 'like the Deity'. God is simple in so far as he is pure and unmixed being. Traherne re-affirms the great dogma of scholasticism:[2] 'God is not a being compoundable of body and soul, or substance and accident, or power and act, but is all act, pure act, a Simple Being whose essence is to be, whose Being is to be perfect so that He is most perfect towards all and in all' (*Centuries*, III, 63). Traherne writes this with all the authority of personal experience. To appreciate the full significance of Traherne's position we must remember that he was writing these words at a time when Aristotelian scholasticism was being derided,[3] and when the tendencies of Puritanism lay in the direction of a separation between matter and spirit,

[1] Op. cit., p. 53.

[2] See Gilson, *The Spirit of Medieval Philosophy*, chapter III, pp. 50 ff., for a full discussion of the medieval conception of God as 'simple' Being.

[3] For instance, by Hobbes, as we have seen, and later by John Dryden in his lines to Dr Charleton (1663). John Webster in his *Academiarum Examen*, 1653, describes Aristotelianism as 'merely verbal, speculative, abstractive, formal and rational, fit to fill the brains with monstrous and airy Chymaeras, speculative and fruitless conceits'.

a division which was absolute, not to be bridged by any human effort.[1] Furthermore this divorce between the worlds of spirit and the worlds of sense which is to be seen in the seventeenth century was re-inforced by the influence of Descartes. For instance Joseph Glanvill, the contemporary of Traherne at Oxford and a follower of Cartesian ideas, points out vividly the difficulties of bridging the gulf between matter in motion and Mind or Soul:

> How the purer Spirit is united to this Clod, is a knot too hard for fallen Humanity to unty. How should a thought be united to a marble statue, or a sun-beam to a lump of clay! The freezing of the words in the air in the northern climes, is as conceivable as this strange union. . . . And to hang weights on the wings of the winds seems more intelligible.[2]

Traherne would agree that this is a mystery but not therefore unintelligible to what he would call the 'highest reason'. There is no difficulty for him because, for the man who has reached the point where mystical illumination is possible, the gulf no longer exists. One must note, too, that Traherne is using criteria that his contemporaries would have approved of. He may use the terms of scholasticism, 'essence, act, power', but his method is that of reflection based upon actual observation; in his case, of his own experiences. The experience of Traherne is that at this moment of illumination, the spirit becomes the clod, the clod becomes the spirit. The spirit is 'the Substance of the Mind':

> The Sense its self was I.
> I felt no Dross nor Matter in my Soul,
> No Brims nor Borders, such as in a Bowl
> We see: My Essence was *Capacity*.

Here then is Traherne living 'this strange union', offering in his own being a solution to the difficulties the analytical reason, working in isolation from fields which it regarded as suspect, was discovering at this period. Traherne feels himself to be a unity, at one with himself and with the world around him, filled with a sense of infinite possibilities. The complete mystic, that is, the man who has reached the fifth stage, adds a further term; he is also at one with God. Traherne does not in these examples exemplify this final stage. He is still in the stage of illumination in so far as he is discovering a reality in himself and in the world around him.

[1] See Tawney, *Religion and the Rise of Capitalism* (London, 1922), pp. 96–8.
[2] Joseph Glanvill, *Vanity of Dogmatizing* (1661), p. 20.

The experience that underlies the two poems *My Spirit* and *The Preparative* is referred to also in the final meditation of the *First Century*. In the poems the infinite and boundless self with its capacity to feel and live the life of other objects provides the main point of emphasis. The inner self, unlike the ordinary daily selves of human society, is complete and single, in Traherne's term, simple. These are the very qualities attributed to God, as I have noted, but Traherne does not, in these poems, proceed therefore to an identification between God and the living endless eye which is his real self. The phrase 'like the Deity' bears no remarkable emphasis. In the prose, however, he is more specific. The self which, in the poems,

> is a Sphere,
> Not limited, but everywhere

is in the prose firmly linked with God. Its infinity is stated to be the infinity of God: 'And thus all Angels and the Eternity and Infinity of God are in me for evermore. I being the living temple of and comprehensor of them' (*Centuries*, I, 100). There is a significant shift of emphasis. The self is infinite as the temple and comprehensor must be, but the infinity of God is paramount; the vehicle must necessarily be secondary. The form of these two sentences indicates in what order emphasis is to be placed on their content. It is not now the self which is regarded as infinite; it is the infinity of God within the self that is now seen to be the real source of the experience which the two poems express. The poems stress the wonder and mystery of the self in this condition,

> . . . so quick and pure
> That all my Mind was wholy Every-where;
> What e're it saw, 'twas actually *there*:[1]
> (*My Spirit*, ll. 54–8)

The prose dwells upon the mystical dwelling of God within the self; 'And thus all ages are present in my soul, and all kingdoms, and God blessed for ever. And thus Jesus Christ is seen in me, and dwelleth in me, when I believed upon Him' (*Centuries*, I, 100). The poetry in this instance is concerned with the power of the soul as able to contain all things within itself. The prose lays emphasis on God as perfect and complete and the cause of perfection wherever it may exist.

A further difference of the same kind is to be noted. In the same poem, *My Spirit*, Traherne writes of the soul as 'all Eye, all Act, all

[1] Op. cit., p. 53.

Sight' (l. 29). In the 84th Meditation of the *Second Century* he writes of God: 'He is all eye and all ear.' I do not suggest that a consistent distinction could be made between the poems and the *Centuries* on these lines, that what, in the poetry, is said of the soul is, in the prose, said of God. I am concerned here with noting a particular phase of the stage of illumination. Both prose and poetry are to be borne in mind for this purpose. What Traherne writes in the *Centuries* must be taken to complete or enlarge what is written in the poetry. One conclusion we may draw is this. Christian thinkers have always hesitated to identify the innermost self with God. Yet the actual experience of the mystics impels them to this very conclusion which the conscious doctrinal mind is reluctant to make, that this secret self, this 'sphere of Light' is also God. (Incidentally, although this is beyond the scope of this essay, this identification is one that other mystical traditions, outside Christianity, for instance that of the *Vedanta*, did not flinch from making.) Traherne feels this identity to be a fact of experience, but evades explicitly saying so by means of these differences we have noted. Furthermore at this moment of experience Traherne is no longer aware of the distinctions implied by terms of location. God is alone perfect and infinite; if the self attains to this state then it becomes like God. God is the source of all things and therefore it is no blasphemy to speak of the soul as infinite and perfect. It is the experience of God which has made it so. Traherne realizes explicitly the futility of attempting to locate God in this way whether inside or outside the self since these terms have only a limited validity. He expresses this realization in this passage which may be considered together with the extracts I have been discussing:

> Whether it be the Soul itself, or God in the Soul, that shines by Love, or both, it is difficult to tell: but certainly the love of the Soul is the sweetest thing in the world. I have often admired what should make it so excellent. If it be God that loves, it is the shining of His essence; if it be the Soul, it is His Image: if it be both, it is a double benefit (*Centuries*, IV, 83).

In either case, Traherne writes, the effects are the same and as we have already noted Traherne maintains the argument of scholasticism that the effect cannot be unlike the cause. If the effect is a state of perfection which for Traherne it is, the cause must partake of the nature of perfection. In the following meditation Traherne goes on to say that not merely is it difficult to say what is the source of this shining illumination, God or the self, or both, but it is impossible to do so.

How is it, he asks, that the soul can possess such power, a power which is equal in its radiance to the light of God shining through his creation? 'If you ask how a Soul that was made of nothing can return so many flames of Love? Where it should have them, or out of what ocean it should communicate them?, it is impossible to declare—(For it can return those flames upon all Eternity, and upon all the creatures and objects in it.)' (*Centuries*, III, 84). Traherne expresses this mystery by the image of the perfect mirror. The inner self, the true self can become a perfect mirror reflecting the light that comes from God: 'For as a looking glass is nothing in comparison of the world, yet containeth all the world in it, and seems a real fountain of those beams which flow from it, so the Soul is nothing in respect of God, yet all Eternity is contained in it, and it is the real fountain of that Love that proceedeth from it' (*Centuries*, IV, 84).

Through his experience of illumination Traherne writes, 'We enter into the heart of the universe' (*Centuries*, I, 56). This experience brings with it for Traherne a sense of participating in universal life from within, 'as if we were God's spies'.[1] It leads to complete and absolute enjoyment. This is the word which is most typical of the man. This enjoyment derives from his certainty that he is no longer simply himself, a separate or detached individual. He is no longer living a life simply in a limited world of time. He lives consciously now at the point of intersection of the world in time with the world which is outside time.

> The rays of our light are by this means darted from everlasting to everlasting. This spiritual region makes us infinitely present with God, Angels, and Men in all places from the utmost bounds of the everlasting hills, throughout all the unwearied durations of His endless infinity, and gives us the sense and feeling of all the delights and praises we occasion as well as of all the beauties and powers and pleasures and glories which God enjoyeth or createth (*Centuries*, V, 9).

The perfect enjoyment which Traherne knows differs from the partial enjoyment of ordinary human life and society in that he feels himself to be actually present in the beings of other individuals and also with infinite and eternal being at the same time: 'The Omnipresence and Eternity of God are your fellows and companions' (*Centuries*, I, 19). The God which Traherne now knows 'is not an Object of Terror, but Delight' (*Centuries*, I, 17). This insistence on the delight and en-

---

[1] *King Lear*, Act V, Sc. iii. 17.

joyment of experiencing the world as in and of God is the distinctive characteristic of Traherne's mysticism. A mystical gaiety, it lies at the centre of his most splendid prose passages:

> You never enjoy the world aright till the Sea itself floweth in your veins, till you are clothed with the heavens, and crowned with the stars: and perceive yourself to be the sole heir of the whole world, and more so, because men are in it who are everyone sole heirs as well as you. Till you can sing and rejoice and delight in God, as misers do in gold, and Kings in sceptres, you never enjoy the world (*Centuries*, I, 29).

This in a special sense is a mystical worldliness. It is the power of enjoying to the full the apparently most trivial details of ordinary life because these details are realized as all part of the universal order. Paradoxically, unless the world is seen *sub specie aeternitatis* it will not yield its full enjoyment. The so-called worldly man who regards the phenomenal world as the only one is never completely satisfied. The knowledge and assurance of a transcendent reality is the firm basis for enjoying the physical world. For then the physical world is known for what it is; its limitations are defined and we are not likely to be deceived by expecting more from it than it can possibly provide. This I take to be an important meaning of the following words from the 16th Meditation of the *First Century*. 'For if you know yourself, or God, or the World, you must of necessity enjoy it.' By knowledge, Traherne means first hand experience; in the following Meditation he writes: 'to know GOD is Life Eternal. . . . To know God is to know Goodness. It is to see the beauty of infinite Love. . . . It is to see the King of Heaven and Earth take infinite delight in *Giving*. Whatever knowledge else you have of God, it is but Superstition.'

Traherne proceeds to define his meaning of 'world'. By world he means not only the round earth on which we live and die and the societies that haunt its surface. He thinks also of time past and time future, of the intangible and infinite intermingling with temporal and physical actuality; but the whole passage is worth quoting:

> The WORLD is not this little Cottage of Heaven and Earth. Though this be fair it is too small a Gift. When God made the World he made the Heavens, and the Heaven of Heavens, and the Angels and the Celestial Powers. These also are parts of the World: So are all those infinite and eternal Treasures that are to abide for ever, after the Day of Judgement. Neither are there some here, and some there but all everywhere, and at once to be enjoyed. The WORLD is unknown, till the Value and Glory of it is seen: till the Beauty and the Serviceableness of its parts is considered. When you enter into it, it is an

illimited field of Variety and Beauty: where you may lose yourself in the multitude of Wonders and Delights. But it is an happy loss to lose oneself in admiration at one's own Felicity; and to find GOD in exchange for oneself. Which we then do when we see Him in His Gifts and adore His Glory (*Centuries*, I, 18).

And as the world, as Traherne sees it, is more than the world of the ordinary observer, so the self which is the object of knowledge is more than the ordinary physical self: 'You never know yourself till you know more than your body. The Image of God was not seated in the features of your face, but in the lineaments of your Soul. In the knowledge of your Powers, Inclinations, and Principles, the knowledge of yourself chiefly consisteth.' Traherne speaks of this real self in the terms which, as we have already noted in this chapter, are applicable also to infinite deity. The powers, inclinations and principles of this self 'are so great that even to the most learned of men, their Greatness is Incredible; and so Divine, that they are infinite in value' (*Centuries*, I, 19). Traherne never directly asserts that this god-like self is identical with divine reality. He does say so, though, indirectly. The very form of the sentence which initiated these observations is significant: 'if you know yourself or God or the World, you must of necessity enjoy it.' We know the sense that Traherne gives to 'World', 'yourself', and 'know'. As he has written this sentence there is in it an implied equivalence between God, World and Yourself. Knowledge of each, that is, direct experience of the spiritual and timeless reality which is in each, will inevitably lead to enjoyment, and enjoyment is the possession of 'Great, Endless, Eternal Delights' (*Centuries*, I, 19). 'You must of necessity enjoy it'—strictly speaking, 'it' could stand for yourself, God or the World. The implication of identity is repeated and I take it to be evidence of Traherne's sense of participation with divine reality. This evidence is empirical. The appeal is always to experience: 'it is an happy loss to lose oneself in admiration at one's own Felicity: and to find GOD in exchange for oneself' (*Centuries*, I, 18).

This is the final test for Traherne; he has experienced perfection; he has known absolute content. There are no anticlimaxes, none of the moments of regret or dejection that follow the ecstasies of the temporal and finite world, however they may be induced: 'I perceive that we were to live the life of God, when we lived the true life of nature according to knowledge' (*Centuries*, III, 58). By 'knowledge' Traherne means participating in the very essence of the object of your contemplation so that 'you are clothed with the heavens and crowned with the stars'. By 'true' he means grounded in reality, not the life of invention or custom, but that which is based on the divinity which is in all things and which is yet transcendent, which is 'of itself'. Having entered upon this life, Traherne writes: 'I was . . . seated in a throne of repose and perfect rest. All things were well. Whereupon you will not believe, how I was withdrawn from all endeavours of altering and mending outward things' (*Centuries*, III, 60). In the same passage Traherne points to the necessity of vigilance; if this enjoyment, and this word belongs to Traherne's most characteristic experience, is to be maintained, the disciplines of amendment must also be maintained. Though according to the *Centuries*, once the vision of God in the world has been known the very experience is a powerful influence in maintaining its continuance; a spiritual momentum is created. Traherne writes of his vision: 'It transforms the Soul and makes it Heavenly . . . it puts a lustre upon God and all His creatures and makes us see them in a Divine and Eternal Light' (*Centuries*, III, 60).

CHAPTER V

Traherne and his Times

IN reading the *Centuries* or the *Poems of Felicity*, one is impressed above all by Traherne's own sense of personal discovery. Where traces of other writers are evident or quotations are inserted, one feels that Traherne is motivated not by the need to find support from authorities but by the enthusiasm and excitement of finding in others the very things he had found for himself in his own experience of life. Traherne is not systematically pursuing any one line of thought or doctrine; it is not possible to say with any confidence in his case that this is derived from such and such a source, or that here one can discern a particular influence at work. Yet quite clearly he had read and studied widely; the Bible, Plato, St Augustine, St Gregory Nazienzen, 'the schools', the *Corpus Hermeticum*, Pico Della Mirandola, Giordano Bruno, all are quoted or referred to.[1] But our sense of Traherne's independence remains.

Although it may be recognized that personal experience is the basis of his doctrine, it is also true that much of this doctrine does illustrate prevailing movements in the thought and sensibility of his time. For instance the antithesis made in Traherne's record of his spiritual history between the natural and pure desires of the child and the world of artifice and contrivance of human society, might well be taken as an illustration of one of the major developments of the seventeenth century. Recent scholarship has continued to be concerned with 'the growing disparity, in the course of the seventeenth century, between the two worlds of the man-made or social and the untouched natural, where these worlds were considered as having philosophical correlatives'.[2]

Similarly Traherne's praise of the simple pure intelligence could be regarded as illustrating the metaphysical grounds of the seventeenth-

---

[1] For instance, his *Commonplace Book*, which is unpublished MS. in the possession of the Dobell family, contains extensive notes from Ficino's translation of Plato's works. See Wade, op. cit., p. 256.

[2] Harold Wendell Smith, 'Nature, Correctness and Decorum', *Scrutiny*, vol. XVII, no. 4, p. 287.

century movement towards the plain, clear, non-metaphorical thought expressed in prose of complete simplicity which Bishop Sprat, for instance, advocates. Traherne's poem *The Person* is relevant in this respect:

> The Naked Things
> Are most Sublime, and Brightest shew,
> When they alone are seen:
> Mens Hands than Angels Wings
> Are truer wealth, tho here below;
> For those but seem.
> Their Worth they then do best reveal,
> When we all Metaphors remove.
> For Metaphors conceal,
> And only Vapors prove.
> They best are blazon'd when we see
> Th' Anatomy,
> Survey the Skin, cut up the Flesh, the Veins
> Unfold:
>
> (ll. 17–30)

In the language of clear, plain, unadorned statement the thing itself will provide its own best glory without the 'crowns and precious stones' of metaphor. In similar phrases Sprat writes with approval of 'the primitive purity, and shortness, when man delivered so many things almost in an equal number of words . . . a close, naked, natural way of speaking, positive expressions, clear senses, a native easiness; bringing all things as near the mathematical plainness as they can'.[1] Whenever Traherne writes of his purity of vision as a child or in the state of self-amendment, it is always as the condition in which his experience seems most real:

> A disentangled and a naked Sense,
> A Mind that's unpossest,
> A disengaged Breast,
> A quick unprejudic'd Intelligence.
>
> (*The Preparative*, ll. 61–4)

This might well be paralleled with Sprat's characteristic concern with the experience of facts without 'engagement', without the entanglement of metaphor.

I am more concerned, however, with drawing attention to the grounds on which Traherne sees Nature as good and human nature as excellent, considering particularly the point in time when Traherne

[1] Sprat, *The History of the Royal Society*, Second Part, Sect. XX.

was writing. This, we should remind ourselves, was the period of the Restoration. Marvell, Dryden and the Cambridge Platonists were his contemporaries as well as the dramatists of the Restoration stage. As we have noted in the previous chapter, Traherne sees the human person both in body and spirit as a living miracle:

> My limbs and members when rightly prized, are comparable to the fine gold, but that they exceed it. The topaz of Ethiopia and the gold of Ophir are not to be compared to them. What diamonds are equal to my eyes; what labyrinths to my ears; what gates of ivory, or ruby leaves to the double portal of my lips and teeth? Is not sight a jewel? Is not hearing a treasure? Is not speech a glory? (*Centuries*, I, 66).

In the same vein Traherne quotes in the *Fourth Century* an extract from the Latin work *Asclepius*, which was part of the body of Hermetic writings that were popular in the sixteenth and seventeenth centuries:[1]

> Man is a great and wonderful miracle. . . . A messenger between the creatures, Lord of inferior things, and familiar to those above; by the keenness of his senses, the piercing of his reasons, and the light of knowledge, the interpreter of nature, a seeming interval between time and eternity, and the inhabitant of both, the golden link or tie of the world, yea, the Hymenaeus marrying the Creator and His creatures together (*Centuries*, IV, 74).

This exalted view of human nature had been accompanied in Elizabethan times and in the early seventeenth century by a sense of man's mortality, of the skull beneath the flesh. In the extract from *Hamlet* with which this essay begins, the two attitudes are sharply opposed. Man, the beauty of the world, the paragon of animals, god-like in apprehension, is, at the same time, the quintessence of dust. The goodly frame of the earth, the brave over-hanging firmament, the majestical roof fretted with golden fire, is also a sterile promontory, a foul and pestilent congregation of vapours. Donne complains bitterly[2] that we who else would be immortal suffer from defects and liabilities from which the rest of creation is free. Renaissance man, for all his magnificence, is yet haunted by the dangers of the sin of pride, the most deadly of the seven. The splendours of nature still contain traces of the poison of original sin. The need for redemption both of man and nature is still felt to be urgent. If the world of *King Lear* has any rele-

---

[1] The *Corpus Hermeticum* appeared in 1471, and 22 editions were issued before 1641. This esoteric collection originated in Egypt probably in the third century A.D. and forms a strange synthesis of Platonic, Neo-Platonic and Stoic theory, Judaic allegory and oriental mythology.

[2] See the sonnet: 'If poisonous minerals, and if that tree', *Holy Sonnets* (1633).

vance to the world of England at the time of its writing, as surely it has, then the play can provide ample illustration of this need; and Lady Macbeth's metaphor of heaven peeping through the blanket of the dark can be seen as expressive of the sense of active supernatural forces operating in the natural world.

Traherne's vision of the world and of man sustains the idea of a spiritual reality shining through the concealing veil of so-called material things. But the sense of humanity as the quintessence of dust is absent. There is, in Traherne, no sense of a forbidden knowledge or of the dangers of trespassing into unlawful fields of experience.[1] The whole world of thought and sense is open to us, to be explored and enjoyed. There are no fatal defects, no corrupting poisons. The only sin is ingratitude to God and ignorance of the beauty of His creation, which, if rightly seen, is perfect and needs no alteration: 'You never enjoy the World aright, till you see all things in it so perfectly yours that you cannot desire them any other way: and till you are convinced that all things serve you best in their proper places' (*Centuries*, I, 38). I take this as a vision of the mystic who receives a vision of man and nature illuminated by divine reality: in this sense, and in this sense only, whatever is, is right. The world of nature and of human nature is redeemed for Traherne by this experience: 'I was (as Plato saith, *In summa rationis arce quies habitat*) seated in a throne of repose and perfect rest. Whereupon you will not believe how I was withdrawn from all endeavours of altering and amending outward things. They lay so well, methought, they could not be mended: but I must be mended to enjoy them' (*Centuries*, III, 60). The gulf between the absolute and the fallen world has been closed at this level of mystical vision.

Similarly, the exaltation of human nature springs from the perception of divinity within the human person. Things are well as they are: humanity can achieve perfection through the very nature that God has created and endowed. For humanity to realize its perfection, its essentially sacred and divine nature must be known and prized:

> Since God is the most Glorious of all Beings, and the most blessed, could'st thou wish any more than to be His IMAGE! O my Soul, He hath made thee His Image. Sing, O Ye Angels, and laud His name, Ye Cherubims: let all the Kingdoms of the Earth be glad, and let all the Host of Heaven rejoice for He hath made His Image, the likeness of Himself, His own similitude. . . . He

---

[1] See *Centuries*, I, 13.

was infinite Love, and being lovely in being so, would prepare for Himself a most lovely object. Having studied for all Eternity, He saw none more lovely than the Image of His Love, His own Similitude (*Centuries*, I, 67).

Traherne's vision is theocentric still: to praise mankind is to praise God. Yet one cannot avoid feeling at times that, for Traherne, to praise God is also to praise mankind. Man is a glorious creature because he reflects divine perfection: he also retains a divinity within himself. We see here not the deification of human personality but the appraisal of the divinity within the human form. We accept Traherne's vision not as complacent optimism therefore but as the declaration of mystical knowledge which the majority of us do not share.

Yet before the end of the seventeenth century similar affirmations of the perfection of creation were to be made as a matter of philosophic argument and reflection, not as the result of mystical experience. We have only to consider the words of John Locke that 'the works of nature in every part of them sufficiently evidence a Deity'.[1] An optimism of acceptance has replaced the vision of the world as paradise. What to Traherne seems a daily miracle now appears the normal features of a natural order which requires no mystical vision for its revelation but simply the operation of reasonableness and good sense:

> The creation is a perpetual Feast to the Mind of a good Man, everything that he sees cheers and delights him; Providence has imprinted so many Smiles on Nature that it is impossible for a mind which is not sunk in more gross and sensual Delights to take a survey of them without several secret Sensations of Pleasure. . . . Natural Philosophy quickens this Taste of the Creation, and renders it not only pleasing to the Imagination, but to the Understanding. It does not rest in the Murmur of Brooks, and the Melody of Birds, in the Shade of Groves and Woods, or in the Embroidery of Fields and Meadows, but considers the several Ends of Providence which are served by them, and the Wonders of Divine Wisdom which appear in them. It heightens the Pleasures of the Eye, and raises such a rational Admiration in Soul as is little inferior to Devotion. . . . Such a habitual Disposition of Mind consecrates every Field and Wood, turns an ordinary walk into a morning and evening Sacrifice and will impose those transient Gleams of Joy which naturally lighten up and reflect the Soul on such occasions into an inviolable and perpetual State of Bliss and Happiness.[2]

These are Addison's words in one of his papers on 'Cheerfulness'.

---

[1] Locke, *Reasonableness of Christianity* (1695). Traherne's words are almost identical: 'Nothing can be but it exhibits a Deity' (*Centuries*, II, 24).
[2] *Spectator* (1712), 393.

Traherne's Felicity has become an 'invisible and perpetual State of Bliss and Happiness'; his vision of man as the meeting point of time and eternity is scaled down into a disposition of mind which 'consecrates every Field and Wood' and 'turns an ordinary walk into a morning or evening sacrifice'. We can see how Traherne's vision of nature differs from the reflections of Addison though both may seem to reach similar conclusions. What is absent from Addison's thoughts is the sense of a mysterious and infinite Godhead inextricably bound up with the fields and woods. The great difference lies in the degree of immediacy of God; to the mystic Traherne, God is immediately present, nearer than we are to ourselves. To Addison God is at one remove; we have, instead, the *tokens* of Providence and of Divine Wisdom. A degree of abstraction has taken place.

One might call the difference that we can see here an example of the recession of God that was taking place in men's minds, and had been going on since Bacon's times and his severance of divinity from the rest of our experience. The world was becoming divided into two halves, the natural and the supernatural, and it is clear from the extract from the *Spectator* that the natural order is becoming sufficient in itself. Furthermore man and not God was becoming the centre of human interest. And man was thought to possess a natural sense of right and wrong, antecedent to, and independent of, any religious beliefs. This is one of the principal themes for instance of Shaftesbury's *Inquiry concerning Virtue or Merit*.[1]

The point of interest concerning the historical position of Traherne is this. On the one hand his view of nature[2] would seem to give support to the typical movement that was to lead to the confidence and optimism of eighteenth-century deism and to the decline in the awareness of a transcendent Deity who was yet the very ground of the existence of the natural world of men and things. On the other hand he can, and I believe should, be regarded as an agent of resistance to this flow of ideas, in so far as he maintains the supremacy of final causes and in so far as his conviction is primarily of a supernatural spiritual reality from which all truth, beauty and goodness must proceed. Man and nature

[1] 1699.
[2] Cf. 'The Heavens were an Oracle and Spake
       Divinity; the Earth did undertake
       The office of a Priest;'
Op. cit., *Dumnesse*, p. 45. *Centuries*, II, 17, 22, 23, 24 and 97, all show Traherne's belief that the sensible world reveals God.

are not perfect in themselves; their worth depends upon the deity who is not to be identified with either. Traherne glorifies man but he would have denied that the proper study of mankind was man. To him a man cannot be isolated from God any more than a reflection can exist without its source. The world of time is involved in eternity and, for Traherne, man's business is to see it 'as one with all Eternity, a part of it, a life within it'. Thus Traherne, though he takes part in the re-habilitation of Nature, yet stands in a certain isolation. He maintains through his mystical experience a balance between God, man, and nature. They are linked together but they are not identical and man's Felicity must lie in the knowledge of all three.

In the world in which he lived this balance was being upset. The humility which is the mark of the mystic when he is extolling human worth with his cry of 'not I, but God in me' was passing. It is as though human nature is prone always to the *hubris* which is the traditional tragic theme. Traherne's mystical belief in the splendid nature of man as a reflection of divine perfection could easily become in the minds of ordinary persons a belief in their own natural goodness as existing independently, without the authority of any divine source.[1] Certainly by the time the deistic rationalism of the Augustans was most in vogue it was increasingly difficult to think of the supernatural as impinging on the natural: 'God had retreated to the position of *primum mobile* and Heaven, no longer concerned in the affairs of men, had ceased to "peep through the blanket of the dark".... As Heaven grew inaccessible man shrank in importance, and having lost his humility with his unique destiny, plumed himself on the infallibility of his social poise ...'[2] and we may add, having lost the sense of himself as the image of God began more and more to assert his own importance on the one hand and yet to become more and more indifferent on the other to the real ground of human dignity.

It might be argued that the Cambridge Platonists contributed in their way to this exclusion of the sense of the supernatural as operating in human affairs, since of all the seventeenth-century moralists their doctrines pointed most clearly towards the elevation of the natural moral sense of man: 'to act aright, they taught, we need but look within, and scan the natural law written upon the heart'.[3] They were

---

[1] 'The supernatural ... was banished from Nature' (referring to the last years of the seventeenth century), B. Willey, *The 18th Century Background*, p. 4.

[2] S. L. Bethell, *Shakespeare and the Popular Dramatic Tradition* (1944), p. 83.

[3] Basil Willey, *The 18th Century Background*, p. 58.

great rationalizers of religious imagery, and the reason, as John Smith[1]
writes, with its 'true understanding of things in their coherence and
contexture' is superior to imagination in attaining to the knowledge of
the real. The understanding must be kept clear of the fiction of metaphor and image. This is the principle maintained by Smith in his
*Discourse, Concerning the True Way or Method of attaining to Divine
Knowledge*, and it is in accord with the intellectual and rationalist
movement of the century. However, Smith must be regarded not as
contributing to the decline of religion in the second half of the seventeenth century, but, like Traherne, moved by a profound desire to
deepen the religious consciousness of the times. Smith, I believe, was a
less advanced mystic than Traherne, if, indeed, one can legitimately
call him one at all; he had less sense of the God who includes infinity
in His nature. But, and in this respect the two men are very similar,
they both insist that knowledge of God comes not by demonstration or through logical argument, but by 'spiritual sensation'.
Religious belief must be founded not upon evidence but upon experience. Moreover the experience of God is given only to those who
have become as little children, that is, to purified and disciplined
spirits.

John Smith died shortly before Traherne's admission to Oxford but
it is possible, as I have suggested, that Traherne may have heard
Whichcote preach or met others of the Platonist group during his
period as chaplain to Sir Orlando Bridgeman. But the point is of little
importance, for what there is in common between Traherne and the
Cambridge Platonists does not depend upon direct contact either in
person or through their writings. The most significant similarity is
their shared conviction that knowledge of God is not to be reached by
abstract theoretical discourse but by immediate experience, by becoming one with God. Traherne wrote of his early intimations of deity
that 'They are unattainable by book and therefore I will teach them by
experience' (*Centuries*, III, 1). 'Is it not strange that an infant should be
heir of the whole world and see those mysteries which the books of
the learned never unfold?' (*Centuries*, III, 2), and he proceeds: 'I will in
the light of my soul show you the Universe' (*Centuries*, III, 6). The
difference between this personal knowledge and the theology of the
schools is expressly made clear by Smith: 'It is but a thin, aiery knowledge that is got by mere Speculation, which is usher'd in by Syllo-
gisms and Demonstrations; but that which springs forth from true

[1] 1618-1652.

Goodness . . . brings such a Divine light into the Soul, as is more clear and convincing than any Demonstration . . .'[1]

The similarity continues: 'Were I to define Divinity', writes Smith, 'I should rather call it a Divine life than a Divine Science; it being something rather to be understood by a Spiritual sensation than by any verbal description.'[2] Traherne thinks of divinity as the practice of God-like thoughts. But by thought Traherne includes the enjoyment and right valuation of things, a right sense of values in the modern phrase: 'To think well is to serve God in the interior court. To have mind composed of Divine Thoughts, and set in frame, to be like Him within. To conceive aright and to enjoy the world is to conceive the Holy Ghost, and to see His Love which is the Mind of the Father' (*Centuries*, I, 10).

> We are like Him when our minds are in frame. Our minds are in frame when our thoughts are like His. And our thoughts are then like His when we have such conceptions of all objects as God hath and prize all things according to their value. For God does prize all things rightly, which is a Key that opens into the very thoughts of His Crown (*Centuries*, I, 13).

Finally, 'It needeth nothing but *the sense of God*[3] to inherit all things. We must borrow and derive it from Him by seeing His, and aspiring after it. Do but clothe yourself with Divine resentments[4] and the world shall be to you the valley of vision. . . .' (*Centuries*, III, 84).

What is remarkable and distinctive in the Traherne extracts here lies in his attempt to define what divine thoughts may be. He agrees with Smith that divinity is to be lived[5] and not simply studied; but he goes further; to be like God one must prize all things according to their value. The act which makes man divine lies in his perception of things as divine. This may seem tautological. The point, I think, is this. God is not simply immanent in a flower. (He is in so far as all things proceed from God.) He resides in the esteeming of it according to its real value. Its real value lies in its revelation of absolute deity which is to be known only when the observer has cleansed 'the gates of perception'. A positive act of liberation is necessary.[6] The divinity will lie hidden in the

---

[1] John Smith, *Discourse I* (1673 ed.), p. 4. [2] Ibid., p. 1. [3] My italics.

[4] (*a*) Feeling or emotion; (*b*) Sensation. Both meanings were common, according to the *N.E.D.*, between 1650 and 1700.

[5] 'To live the life of God is to live to all the Works of God and to enjoy them in His Image' (*Centuries*, III, 13).

[6] 'Unless it (i.e. the soul) will up and think and taste and see all is in vain' (*Centuries*, IV, 95).

world of objects until the individual releases it. God is always there but not known until enjoyed. We are of course faced with a logical difficulty. What is the order of precedence? Does knowing or esteeming come first? Do we ever know what the 'right' valuation of any object is prior to its supreme 'enjoyment'? In all the relevant passages in Traherne, 'enjoy' and 'know' are used in a way which suggests that the two words are identical in meaning for him in dealing with the experience he wishes to communicate. There is a simultaneous realization. The object is rightly valued when the subject 'knows' it, that is, participates in and rejoices in its life. Subject and object are merged in a unity which is included in the absolute reality from which all subjects and objects proceed. 'God is the object and God is the way of enjoying' (*Centuries*, V, 1).

This divine life can be realized here and now in the world of time and sense. Both Traherne and Smith make this affirmation.

> To seek our Divinity merely in Books and Writings, is *to seek the living among the dead*. We do but in vain seek God many times in these, where his Truth too often is not so much enshrin'd but entomb'd: no; *intra te quaere Deum*, seek for God within thine own soul; he is best discern'd νοεϱὰ επαψὲ, as *Plotinus* phrased it, by an intellectual touch of him: we must see with our eyes, and hear with our ears, and our hands must handle the word of life. . . . David, when he would teach us how to know what the divine Goodness is, calls not for Speculation but Sensation, 'Taste and see how good the Lord is.'[1]

Traherne quotes the Psalms[2] in precisely the same way: 'By all which we may see what inwards life we ought to lead with God in the Temple. And that to be much in the meditation of God's works, and laws, to see their excellency, *to taste their sweetness, to behold their glory, to advise and rejoice and overflow* with praises is to live in Heaven.'[3] And Traherne proceeds: 'But unless we have a communion with David in a rational knowledge of their nature and excellency, we can never understand the grounds of his complacency, or depth of his resentments' (*Centuries*, III, 92).

In this way both Traherne and Smith identify religious knowledge with religious experience; the idea of God must be realized in the world of phenomena. Every man must make God real by becoming like God himself. It follows that in a real sense Heaven can be experienced in the world. The world is divine, and when error and ignorance are dispersed

---

[1] John Smith, *Discourse I* (1673 ed.), p. 3.
[2] Both men have Psalm 119 in mind. [3] My italics.

there is nothing to prevent the direct enjoyment of the presence of God. Heaven is not only a place but a state of being. Similarly the Devil is not so much a local presence as a principle of evil: 'When we say, The Devil is continually busie with us, I mean not only some Apostate spirit as one particular Being, but that Spirit of Apostasie which is lodged in all men's natures; as the Scripture speaks of Christ not only as a Particular person but as a Divine Principle in Holy Souls.'[1] Traherne writes in the same way:

> Tis not change of place, but glorious principles well practised that establish Heaven in the life and soul. An Angel will be happy anywhere, and a devil miserable, because the principles of the one are always good, of the other, bad. From the centre to the utmost bounds of the everlasting hills all is Heaven before God, and full of treasure; and all that walks like God in the midst of them, blessed (*Centuries*, IV, 37).

For Traherne Heaven is identified with Felicity, the knowledge that 'All Things are infinitely beautiful in their places, and wholly yours in all their places'. To be in Heaven is 'to have blessings and to prize them' (*Centuries*, I, 47), and, he continues, 'To prize blessings while we have them is to enjoy them, and the effect thereof is contentation, pleasure, thanksgiving, happiness' (*Centuries*, I, 47). In this sense Heaven is not a future state nor Hell an exclusively posthumous locality; both may be enjoyed or suffered here and now. The state of Hell may be experienced as that of being in Heaven without realizing it, as a Hell of ignorance and lost opportunity. Traherne writes of a Hell on earth and of a Hell in, presumably, an after life when the sensible blessings of this world are no longer available: 'To have blessings and to prize them is to be in Heaven; to have them and not to prize them is to be in Hell, I would say upon Earth; To prize them and not to have them, is to be in Hell' (*Centuries*, I, 47). This conception of Heaven and Hell is indeed what we should expect from Traherne's preoccupation not with time but with eternity. There is for Traherne an eternal now. Eternity does not lie in a world of 'ever after'. If to be in Heaven is to see the world as God sees it, then the experience of Heaven is for him a perpetual possibility in the so-called world of time. For time has no separate existence or reality in Traherne's experience: 'Time itself being in God eternally' (*Centuries*, III, 65). Eternity is not time continued to infinity, an endless succession of to-morrows. That would be to think of eternity in terms of time. On the contrary Traherne apprehends time,

[1] John Smith, op. cit., p. 451.

and indeed infinity also, as included within the nature of God. If Heaven is the experience of God, then heaven is to be realized in the present world since God is omnipresent and eternal.

Sin becomes for Traherne and for Smith a defection from the divine order. It lies in an ignorance of, or a refusal to participate in, the nature of goodness which is everywhere evident: 'God is but One and his Name One . . . and where we find Wisdom, Justice, Loveliness, Goodness, Love and Glory in their highest elevations and most unbounded dimensions. That is He: and when we find any true participations of these there is a true Communication of God; and a defection from these is the Essence of Sin and the Foundation of Hell.'[1] Traherne writes of sin in the same way, although in his ecstatic state he thinks it incredible for anyone, once having known God, to turn away: 'No man can sin that clearly seeth the beauty of God's face: because no man can sin against his own happiness, that is, none can when he sees it clearly, willingly, and wittingly forsake it, tempter, temptation, loss and danger being all seen' (*Centuries*, II, 97). Man can be without sin, can achieve perfection, that is; sin is personal and voluntary.[2] The individual has the power of choice. 'For we may sin or we may be holy' (ibid.). The sure guide to follow in avoiding sin is the conviction that the world is the sacred trust and inheritance of man. That we are the heirs of the world is the thought that echoes ceaselessly in the pages of Traherne. 'Holiness therefore and righteousness *naturally flow out of our fruition of the World*,[3] for who can vilify and debase himself by any sin, while he actually considers he is the heir of it. It exalts a man to a sublime and honourable life: it lifts him above lusts and makes him angelical' (*Centuries*, II, 97). We see here once again the ground of Traherne's belief in the natural goodness of the world of sense perception; it lies in his conception of the world as the unspoilt gift of God: 'the land we tread on is of His munificence' (ibid., 96). All things are sacred in Traherne's vision, therefore, in a world seen as the repository of goodness containing both 'the seeds of Grace and the seeds of Glory' (ibid.). We have in this further illustration of Traherne's view of religion as extending to all aspects of man's being and his activity in human society. We must remark also that to be the heir of the world is not a privilege of a particular individual or of his private contemplations. Felicity is open to us all if we so wish, as Traherne is never tired of

---

[1] John Smith, op. cit., p. 454.
[2] This doctrine is close to the Pelagian heresy. See Chapter IX.
[3] My italics.

affirming: 'All which you have here. GOD, THE WORLD, YOURSELF, ALL THINGS in Time and Eternity being the objects of your Felicity, God The Giver and you the receiver' (*Centuries*, II, 100).

There is nothing here of the dualism between body and spirit, or between the world of nature and that of supernature the growth of which this period of the seventeenth century was witnessing. It will be relevant to remark R. H. Tawney's view when he writes:

> In emphasizing that God's Kingdom is not of this world, Puritanism did not always escape from the suggestion that this world is no part of God's Kingdom. The complacent victim of that false antithesis between the social mechanism and the life of the spirit, which was to tyrannize over English religious thought for the next two centuries, it enthroned religion in the privacy of the individual soul, not without some sighs of sober satisfaction at its abdication from society.[1]

If we accept this then Traherne stands in complete opposition to the 'false antithesis'. For Traherne there is no categorical separation between this world and the next; time is not parallel with eternity: 'It ought to be a firm principle rooted in us, that this life is the most precious season in all Eternity, because all Eternity dependeth on it. *Now*[2] we may do those actions which hereafter we shall never have occasion to do' (*Centuries*, IV, 93). This world is to be made one with the life of Heaven 'as one with all Eternity, a part of it, a life within it'. Traherne thus stands opposed to the tendencies of Puritanism as they are so defined. God's Kingdom can be realized here and now. His mystical vision is stronger than the influences which his residence at Brasenose and his other Puritan connections earlier in his life may have had upon him. Here again we may see how Traherne, and in this I would place him with the Cambridge Platonists, stands in isolation amongst the changes in religious thought and feeling that were gathering momentum in the latter half of the seventeenth century. Traherne sees the whole of human life and the life of nature as in its several degrees essentially sacred; and it was in fact this very view of life that was in process of change:

> If we have in mind merely the intellectual changes of the period we are considering, they have been described by one historian under the title, *La crise de la conscience européenne* a title which itself gives some indication of the importance of the change that was taking place. What was in question was a

---

[1] R. H. Tawney, *Religion and the Rise of Capitalism*, p. 254.
[2] My italics.

colossal secularization of thought in every possible realm of ideas at the same time.[1]

The mystical illumination of Traherne offers a challenge to this secularization of thought. Furthermore one might argue that, in so far as the movement is linked with the development of a sense of the autonomy of the human reason, Traherne is saved from it by the very nature of his own conception of reason. Reason itself for Traherne is divine, that element in us which participates in the eternal mind. Its proper end is God. I have noted already[2] the meaning which Traherne gives to reason and understanding. Some further instances may be given here: 'Nazienzen professed himself to be a lover of right reason, and by it did undertake even to speak oracles. Even so may we by the Reason discover all the mysteries of heaven' (*Centuries*, IV, 81). 'For God gave man an endless intellect to see all things' (*Centuries*, III, 42), and in the *Fourth Century* Traherne writes of 'the infinite extent of the understanding' (*Centuries*, IV, 100). There are no insuperable frontiers then between the province of faith and that of reason. Traherne's view contradicts the distinctions made by Francis Bacon that there is a truth of religion and a truth of science, and the two should be kept separate. This distinction has no validity for Traherne. Reason can approach the mysteries of God and knowledge will lead also to the life of God. It is by 'the highest reason' that Traherne recaptures the miraculous vision of the world that his childhood intuitions first revealed. The mystical life is also the reasonable life; reason will lead to the ultimate mystery.

This high value placed upon reason by Traherne is a further link between him and the Cambridge Platonists. The Platonists are celebrated for their appeals to 'Reason', and reason, as Whichcote repeatedly declares, is 'the candle of the Lord'. The importance of reason lies above all in its quality as the exemplar in the human being of divine perfection. As John Smith writes, our minds 'are so framed as not to admit of any other than *One Infinite* source of all that Reason and Understanding which themselves partake of, in which they live, move and have their Being',[3] and a little later we read, 'He is . . . the *Eternal Reason*, that Almighty *Mind* and Wisdom which our Understandings converse with.'[4] Smith is arguing that the existence of

[1] H. Butterfield, *The Origin of Modern Science* (London, 1950), pp. 166–7. (The historian in question is Paul Hazard, and the book was published in Paris in 1935.)
[2] Chapter II.
[3] J. Smith, op. cit., pp. 118 ff.   [4] Ibid., p. 132.

reason in man presupposes a Supreme Reason existing apart from the individual, Traherne is not concerned with proving the existence of God so much as pointing out how we may find union with Him. This passage however will illustrate clearly how, like Smith, he thinks of God as Eternal Reason:

> He is one infinite Act of KNOWLEDGE and WISDOM. . . . And we are to grow up into Him till we are filled with the fulness of His Godhead. We are to be conformed to the Image of His Glory: till we become the resemblance of His great exemplar, which we then are, when our power is converted into Act, and covered with it, we being an Act of KNOWLEDGE as He is: When our Souls are present with all objects, and beautified with the ideas and figures of them all. For then shall we be MENTES as He is MENS. We being of the same mind with Him who is an infinite eternal mind (*Centuries*, II, 84).

This is the ground for the great value to be put on reason; it is that in us by which we may participate in eternal and infinite mind. This is the ground too, as we have noted, for Traherne's whole praise of human nature and the absence in his writings of any real sense of original sin. By reason, then, Traherne does not mean the human reason regarded as an isolated and autonomous human faculty. It is nothing less than the divine spark within us. In other words, reason for Traherne is directly opposed to the conception we find of it in Hobbes. In the work of Hobbes there is an 'arrogant assertion of the unlimited power of human reason'.[1] Reason as Hobbes sees it has a human reference; it brings to man knowledge and, as he asserts, 'the end of Knowledge is Power'. By contrast Traherne sees reason as one of the means by which man is conformed to 'the Image of His Glory'. This final cause is always present in Traherne's thoughts. The glory of God is the true end to which all human activities should be directed, not sacrificed indeed, but ordered in a 'noble subservience'.

Traherne's use of the term reason in this sense puts him with the Cambridge Platonists in his own day, but I do not regard his platonism as providing his distinctive quality as a mystic. His platonism belongs to a narrower and more circumscribed level of his experience. There are other and more profound considerations to be reckoned with. Traherne the Platonist is concerned with becoming one with God who is eternal mind. Traherne the mystic is united with God as the ground of total being. In the passages which contain the essential mysticism of

---

[1] H. Fisch, 'Bacon and Paracelsus', *The Cambridge Journal*, vol. V, no. 12, p. 756.

the man, the sense of participating in and enjoying the very life of the universe, there is, as I have already suggested, more in common with the medieval realism of Aquinas. The division that Traherne makes as a Platonist between the world and the idea of the world does not reflect his most distinctive characteristics. For instance, he writes that 'the thought of the World whereby it is enjoyed is better than the World. So is the idea of it in the Soul of Man better than the World in the esteem of God' (*Centuries*, II, 90). This is to give to the act of thinking a supreme importance. It points to a distinction between thought as an activity of the mind, and the object about which the activity is centred, and prefers the former: 'a Thought of the World, or the World in a Thought is more excellent than the World, because it is spiritual and nearer unto God. The material world is dead and feeleth nothing . . .' (*Centuries*, II, 90). We must join ourselves with God by forming an idea of the world in our minds, and thus repeat the act of thought by which the universe exists in the mind of God: 'We shall be Mentes as he is Mens.'

This idealist position is the result of a conscious intellectual activity. A reality which is divine has been recognized, in this instance, as an 'infinite eternal Mind'. The individual remains fully conscious of himself as a thinking separate entity; mind converses with mind. The full union with God has not been realized. God is still thought of as possessing qualities and attributes and the individual mystic is still aware of himself as a conscious reflective being. A mind which is busy in the voluntary and intellectual activity with which the material and dead world is sustained in a permissive existence cannot be in the state of selflessness and alert passivity, the state of unknowing in which alone God may be experienced. The thought of God will exclude God; so also the conception of God as an infinite mind will impede union with the absolute unqualified Godhead. These passages show quite clearly that Traherne is here still the thinking self which, no less than the feeling and imagining self, must die away in the experience of the fourth and final stage of purification. He is not, that is, writing of the experience of a contemplative at all. It is the result of discursive meditation, rather, that we see in this.

What can be called mystical in Traherne is contained in his sense of being 'clothed with the heavens, and crowned with the stars'. This is not the result of a conscious intellectual act. It supervenes after the last descent into the abyss of humility, after a surrender of the self to the world of sensible objects, and perhaps this sense was felt but rarely in

his life, in his adult life, that is. In this condition Traherne never speaks
of the material world as dead and devoid of feeling as he does in the
'platonist' passage; nor indeed does he speak of 'mind', but prefers
rather to use the term 'understanding', which he approximates to 'soul'
or 'spirit': 'An act of the understanding is the presence of the Soul,
which being no body but a living Act, is a pure spirit and mysteriously
fathomless in its true dimension' (*Centuries*, II, 76). In this mystical
vision the world of matter is alive with God's presence: 'His greatness
is the presence of His Soul with all objects in infinite space: and His
brightness the light of Eternal Wisdom. His essence also is the Light of
Things. For He is all eye and all ear' (*Centuries*, II, 94).

Perhaps we may see here an instance of the influence of his historical
position on Traherne. He was living at a time when the claims of the
inner light, the individualism of the conscience was in full conflict with
those forces in Church and State which upheld a sanctity transcending
the individual. Furthermore Traherne lacked the benefits of the discipline of a definite mystical tradition, with its safeguards and reserva-
tions. In the midst of the various intellectual and religious tendencies of
his times, it is perhaps not surprising that Traherne, while holding fast
to his essential vision, should have turned at times in a direction which
a more closely instructed mind, or a more systematic one, might have
recognized as leading away from the very consummation which is
sought. The preference for the thought of the world as a creation of the
mind, over the world apprehended as itself spiritual and containing
within itself the seeds of Felicity, is an instance of the discontinuity one
finds between Traherne the orthodox pious High Churchman and
Traherne the 'illuminated' man. God may be known as 'eternal mind',
but he is also 'all eye and all ear', and mystical experience must em-
brace God as both before moving to the ultimate union with a being
who is antecedent to both. Whenever he writes of his mystical experience, Traherne speaks of God not as mind but as a simple and
unmixed being,[1] as a unity in which thought and matter exist without
confusion. All things are contained within the Godhead who is the
terminus of the mystical life.

Where the Platonist in Traherne joins with the mystic is in the enlarged meaning which he clearly gives at times to the terms 'thought'
and 'mind'. Knowledge for Traherne is identical with enjoyment in

[1] '. . . God is not a being compounded of body and soul, or substance and
accident, or power and act, but is all act, pure act, a Simple Being whose essence
is to be, whose Being is to be perfect' (*Centuries*, III, 63).

relation to his mystical experience. So likewise does mind, the divine mind, acquire in the same conditions the meaning of love: 'To have a mind composed of Divine Thoughts, and set in frame, to be like Him within. To conceive aright and to enjoy the world, is to conceive the Holy Ghost, and *to see His Love which is the Mind of the Father*'[1] (*Centuries*, I, 10). In the words of Dean Inge, 'In the *Phaedrus* as in I *Corinthians*, love is the great hierophant of the divine mysteries, which forms the link between divinity and humanity.'[2] It is this 'great hierophant' that I propose to discuss in the following chapter.

[1] My italics.
[2] W. R. Inge, *The Platonic Tradition in English Religious Thought* (London, 1926), p. 13.

CHAPTER VI

The Great Hierophant

THE final end of mystical experience is a union between the individual and the divine reality which is the ground of all being. Logically therefore the individual mystic might be said to be identified with God, to become God indeed at this point. Yet although we may think of the words of William Blake:

> If thou humblest Thyself thou humblest Me.
> Thou also dwellest in eternity.
> Thou art a man. God is no more.
> Thine own humanity learn to adore.[1]

most Christian mystics have been reluctant to make the assertion that man is God in such unqualified terms. Traherne's praise of humanity is in fact and in expression an adoration of divinity. We have seen how in the prose of Traherne the magnificence of human nature derives from the reflection of deity within it and from its actual participation in a divine order. The sense of identity with God is spoken of by Traherne with the same positiveness. He prefers, however, to express this sense in terms of love. He writes certainly of the human being in mystical communion 'as God' conversing 'with God for evermore' (*Centuries*, II, 86), but this, as I have noted, is the characteristic language of illumination, the third stage. In writing of his sense of union with God it is invariably the phraseology of love that Traherne employs.

Traherne sees the whole universal order as a manifestation of infinite and eternal love: 'Every spire of grass is the work of His hand' (*Centuries*, III, 61). 'The very end for which God made the World was that He might manifest His Love' (*Centuries*, II, 62). His vision of Love grows to transcendental dimensions. Love, for Traherne, is the 'force which through the green fuse drives the flower' and he would have thought it perfectly fitting to speak of the Newtonian system in terms of the love of one object for another. It is the power which binds the universe together, and the universe is both physical and spiritual. Love

---

[1] W. Blake, *Poetical Works*, ed. W. B. Yeats (London, 1910), 'The Everlasting Gospel', p. 113.

is a necessity as inevitable as hunger or thirst. The individual whether he chooses to recognize this truth or not is inescapably a part of this manifestation. To realize this is his supreme happiness: it is to realize the truth of his own nature:

> things unknown have a secret influence on the soul, and like the centre of the earth unseen violently attract it. We love we know not what, and therefore everything allures us. As iron at a distance is drawn by the loadstone, there being some invisible communications between them, so is there in us a world of Love to somewhat, though we know not what in the world that should be. There are invisible ways of conveyance by which some great thing doth touch our souls, and by which we tend to it. Do you not feel yourself drawn by the expectation and desire of some Great Thing? (*Centuries*, I, 2).

Man is the heir of this love though he may well be unaware of it, and the purpose of his existence is to enjoy his inheritance: 'The end for which you were created is that by prizing all that God hath done, you may enjoy yourself and Him in Blessedness' (*Centuries*, I, 12). That the world[1] is to be enjoyed is an instance of the love of God; therefore to enjoy the world to the full is to respond fully to the creative act by which both the individual and the world exist at all. Nothing is more pleasing to God than the enjoyment of the world as Traherne apprehends it: 'Which (*sc*. the World) being made to be enjoyed, nothing can please or serve Him more, than the Soul that enjoys it. For that Soul doth accomplish the end of His desire in Creating it' (*Centuries*, I, 10). This world that has no other purpose but to be enjoyed is unknown 'till the Value and Glory of it is seen: till the Beauty and the Serviceableness of its parts is considered' (*Centuries*, I, 18). It is unknown, that is, until it is enjoyed. Its fruition lies in its knowledge when this knowledge is real, that is, apprehended as a manifestation of God. This identification of knowledge and enjoyment is a distinctive fact of Traherne's mysticism of which we have noted frequent instances.

This knowledge which lies in the perception of the world as Heaven and of yourself as the sole heir, and yet of all other selves as the sole heirs as well, is closely linked with Traherne's vision of love. Love, enjoyment and knowledge form a trinity of meaning in Traherne's mystical experience. The words seem to stand for distinct activities which converge in the unity of this experience. Love is a mode of knowledge at this point, a means of knowing God: it provides 'a Gate,

---

[1] We must remember that by 'world' Traherne means also that which transcends 'this little cottage of Heaven and Earth' both in time and space; a supra-sensible reality. See *Centuries*, I, 18.

in the prospect even of this world, whereby you may see into God's Kingdom' (*Centuries*, II, 27). But love is more than knowledge or enjoyment; it is not of equal but of superior status. Love is the medium by which both knowledge and enjoyment become perfect, the very means by which at the moment of perfection God is realized in the world:

> Love is the true means by which the world is enjoyed. Our love to others and others' love to us. We ought therefore above all things to get acquainted with the nature of Love. For love is the root and foundation of nature. Love is the Soul of Life and Crown of rewards. If we cannot be satisfied in the nature of love we can never be satisfied at all (*Centuries*, II, 62).

Traherne clearly gives great importance to his vision of the creative and perfective power of love; it is for him an essentially active and positive force. It is that by which we grow to our full stature; in the language of scholasticism which Traherne uses whenever he is profoundly moved by his experience, it is through love that we become in act what we are in power, that our full nature is realized: 'By Loving a Soul does propagate and beget itself. By Loving it does dilate and magnify itself. By Loving it does enlarge and delight itself. . . . But above all by Loving it does attain itself' (*Centuries*, II, 40). 'Love also being the end of Souls which are never perfect till they are in act what they are in power' (*Centuries*, II, 48). The final step in this series is the realization of the presence of divine reality which is coincident with the perfection of the self. Both events are complete through love. When the individual has attained himself the divinity within him is realized: 'God is present by Love alone' (*Centuries*, II, 50).

Here we may see explicitly the positive nature of Traherne's mysticism. He does not wait for the ray of light which is the love of God to pierce the cloud of unknowing into which a difficult process of purification has brought him. Love to Traherne is an activity, a co-operative activity. It involves above all the awareness of an object other than the individual self, an object existing outside, and apart from, the self. The search for an object which shall satisfy the natural and instinctive demands of the self has for Traherne the inevitability of a law of life. Without love and the sense of objective causes, persons or things which love in its need for giving demands, the spirit will wither and die: souls 'till they love . . . are desolate, without their objects, and narrow and futile, and dishonourable; but when they shine by love upon all objects, they are accompanied with them and enlightened by them. Till we become all Act as God is, we can never rest, nor ever be satisfied' (*Centuries*, II, 48). The individual person needs an object to love for his very spiritual existence. Not only will the soul without love be unable to realize its full development, which is to become 'All Act as God is', but its own death will inevitably result: 'The Soul is shrivelled up and buried in a grave that does not love' (*Centuries*, II, 50). One may compare these words with those of John Tauler: 'He who dwelleth not in love is dead.'[1] (Incidentally, Traherne writes on more than one occasion of the mystic as the friend of God: 'All his care being to be sensible of God's mercies, and to behave himself as the friend of God in the Universe' (*Centuries*, IV, 41) and again later in the same century: 'Our friendship with God ought to be so pure . . . we should even in public endeavour to know Him' (*Centuries*, IV, 93). It was by the title of the Friends of God that John Tauler and his followers were known in Strasbourg and the Rhineland in the fourteenth century. It was a movement that had much in common with the Quakers in the seventeenth century except that the earlier group kept within the orthodoxy of the Church. I do not suggest that Traherne was necessarily consciously using a phrase having in mind these German mystics. The notion of friendship is appropriate to the immediate and concrete relationship which the mystic experiences. But it is an instance of the similarity of expression and, presumably, of experience which mystics separate in time and place reveal.)

Love is the means by which the soul attains its real self. But this real self, is it also God? Traherne does indeed imply this by his use of the third term, love. Where love is, there also is God, for 'God is love, and by loving, he begot His love. He is of Himself, and by loving He is what He is, INFINITE LOVE. God is not a mixt and compounded Being, so that His Love is one thing and Himself another: but the most pure and simple of all Beings, all Act, and pure Love in the abstract' (*Centuries*, IV, 39). Love is indivisible, that is. Again we may think of the words of Tauler in the first paragraph of his *Following of Christ* . . . 'God is a being withdrawn from creatures, a free power, a pure working.' Both mystics here are filled with the vision of the divine reality as essentially one, a fundamental simplicity, not a collection of parts. This notion of God as simple, as a unity, is reiterated throughout the *Centuries*. Traherne proceeds to his most direct statement of the union of the individual self with God in this way, through the presence of

[1] John Tauler (1300–1361), *Sermons*, Winkworth's trans. (London, 1906), p. 294.

Love: 'Love', he writes, 'is the darling of God, I may almost say the God of God. . . . *And this Love is your true self*[1] when you are in act what you are in power' (*Centuries*, IV, 67). This true self is Love and Love is God; but this equation holds only for the individual self who has become in act what he is in power, who has become his true self. At this point the finite individual participates in the nature of the infinite reality, that is, ceases to be finite. The perfection of man's nature which comes about through love comes therefore through God. By the actualization of his own nature man is made a perfect image of God, for this, as Traherne repeatedly asserts, is of the essential nature of man.

By love we become united with God: 'In Him you feel, in Him you live. . . . He hath obliged you to love Him. And if you love Him you must of necessity be Heir of the World, for you are happy in Him. . . . In God you are crowned, in God you are concerned. In Him you feel, in Him you live, and move, and have your being' (*Centuries*, I, 52). If God is the cause of love, it is through his love for us that we love God. Love of God then would seem to mean for Traherne both our love for God and God's love for us. Both meanings are present together. It is through this love that Traherne sees his noblest vision of mankind: 'Are not all His treasures yours, and yours His? Is not your very Soul and Body His: is not His life and felicity yours: is not His desire yours? is not His will yours?. . . . God is yours and the whole world. You are His and you are all; or in all, and with all' (*Centuries*, I, 53).

But is not this an affirmation of pantheism? If you are all, and you are identified with God, is this not to make God simply the sum total of all things? This, however, is a criticism of Traherne's mode of expression rather than of his substantial thought. His mysticism is not fundamentally pantheistic; God is love, but that love is God is true only of the mystical experience. God is of Himself; as He includes infinity in His nature[2] so also he includes infinite love. God is beyond definition although he may be experienced and enjoyed as love. Since God is 'of Himself' he is not therefore simply identical with all things; the universe is within God, not identical with Him: 'All objects are in God eternal: which we by perfecting our faculties are made to enjoy' (*Centuries*, III, 68). The God who is love in Traherne's vision is none the less the transcendent deity who is beyond nature and beyond human conceptions or images of what is God.

---

[1] My italics.
[2] 'Almighty power includes infinity in its own existence' (*Centuries*, V, 4).

I have remarked in several instances already the connection between Traherne's thought and that of medieval philosophy. Nowhere is the connection so close as in what he writes of love, in particular of the relation of self-love to the love of God. Traherne maintains that before love for other men or for God is possible self-love must first be satisfied. Self-love is natural and reasonable and will lead to the love of God for His own sake, the proper end of human activity. 'So that self-love is the basis of all love. But when we do love ourselves and self-love is satisfied infinitely in all its desires and possible demands, then it is easily led to regard the Benefactor more than itself, and for His sake overflows abundantly to all others' (*Centuries*, IV, 55).

Traherne upholds the essential truth of this by asserting that the love of the self for the self is a mystical analogue of the love of God for Himself:

> the reason why He loves Himself being because He is Love, nothing is more glorious than His self-love. For He loves Himself because He is infinite and eternal Love to others. Because He loves Himself He cannot endure that His love should be displeased. And loving others vehemently and infinitely all the love He bears to Himself is tenderness towards them. All that wherein He pleaseth Himself is delightful to them: He magnifieth Himself in magnifying them. And in fine, His love unto Himself is His love unto them, and His love unto them is love unto Himself. They are individually one, which it is very amiable and beautiful to behold, because therein the simplicity of God doth evidently appear.... You must love after His similitude (*Centuries*, IV, 65).

We must love ourselves 'after His similitude' and God's love seeks always His own glory. This is so because His glory is the end of all things: 'God doth desire glory as His sovereign end, but true glory ... true glory is to love another for his own sake, and to prefer his welfare and to seek his happiness, which God doth because it is true glory. So that He seeks the happiness of Angels and Men as His last end, and in that His glory: to wit His true Glory' (*Centuries*, IV, 64). In this sense self-love is the basis of all love because the very cause that love exists at all rests in God's love for Himself.

In the *First Century* Traherne writes that desires

> are the bands and cements between God and us.... Wants are the ligatures between God and us, the sinews that convey Senses from him unto us, whereby we live in Him and feel His enjoyments. For had we not been obliged by having our wants satisfied, we should not have been created to

love Him. And had we not been created to love Him we could never have
enjoyed His eternal Blessedness (*Centuries*, I, 51).

This emphasis that Traherne places on the physical and natural love
of the self for itself, on the very fact of desire as linked with and leading
to the love of God points to a resemblance between his mysticism and
the doctrines of Christian love that St Bernard (1090–1153) and his
disciples developed in the twelfth century. This Cistercian mysticism
as it is sometimes termed, finds its most concise expression in the text
De Diligendo Deo[1] and the *Epistola de Caritate*,[2] both works of St
Bernard. St Bernard holds that between love of God and love of self
there is a profound identity. The two loves constitute an expression of
what is basically the same appetite, 'the deepest and most natural of all,
or better still, the only natural one'.[3] St Bernard affirms that a man's love
'begins necessarily with himself' and that the natural result of this self-
love is to lead to the enjoyment of God, 'as if in wondrous wise he
should forget himself and, as if delivered from self, should be wholly
God's'.[4] The teaching of the *De diligendo Deo* states that it is natural for
man to begin by loving himself, because of the very conditions of our
infirm and feeble nature. The love of ourselves for our own sake, which
St Bernard terms *amor carnalis*, is the starting point for all subsequent
development of love. To love God which is the purpose of all human
life, we must first live, and to live we must love ourselves; '*Sed quoniam
natura fragilior atque infirmior est, ipsi primum imperante necessitate,
compelletur inservire; et est amor carnalis, quo ante omnia homo diligit
seipsum propter seipsum.*'[5] In Traherne's words, 'self-love is the basis
of all love'.

How does the love of the self lead to the love of God? Traherne's
argument is that love is necessary for any object or activity to be
pleasing. To love anything is in a profound sense to be pleasing to God,
to return in some degree the love which proceeds from Him. To love
oneself is to love a member of God's creation and is therefore directed
towards God;

> From His love all the things in Heaven and Earth flow into you; but if you
> love neither Him nor them, you bereave yourself of all, and make them

---

[1] 1126.   [2] 1125.

[3] P. Rousselot, *Pour l'histoire de l'amour au moyen age*; pp. 1–4 quoted by E. Gilson in *The Spirit of Medieval Philosophy*, p. 290.

[4] St Bernard, *De Diligendo Deo, Opera Omnia* (*Patrologiae Latinae*, ed. J.-P.
Migne, Paris, 1862, Tome CLXXXII), vol. I, chap. XV, para. 39, col. 998.

[5] Ibid., chap. VIII, para. 23, col. 988.

infinitely evil and hurtful to you. So that upon your love naturally depends your own excelling and the enjoyment of His. It is by your love that you enjoy all His delights, and are delightful to Him (*Centuries*, IV, 48).

Traherne continues in a manner which we have noticed already as characteristic of him. He apprehends a universe in which the members depend upon and yet explain each other. Through the finite, or the less complete, the infinite is reached:

> It is very observable by what small principles infusing them in the beginning God attaineth infinite ends. By infusing the principle of self-love He hath made a creature capable of enjoying all worlds; to whom, did he not love himself, nothing could be given. By infusing grateful principles and inclinations to thanksgiving He hath made the creature capable of more than all worlds, yea, of more than enjoying the Deity in a simple way: though we should suppose it to be infinite.

The 'small' principle of self-love leads to the higher love. Traherne insists that this is so as a fact of experience:

> For to enjoy God as the fountain of infinite treasures, and as the giver of all, is infinite pleasure; but He by His wisdom infusing grateful principles, hath made us upon the very account of self-love to love Him more than ourselves. And us, who without self-love could not be pleased at all, even as we love ourselves, He hath so infinitely pleased, that we are able to rejoice in Him, and to love Him more than ourselves. And by loving Him more than ourselves, in very gratitude and honour, to take more pleasure in His felicity, than in our own, by which way we best enjoy Him. To see His wisdom, goodness and power employed in creating all worlds for our enjoyment, and infinitely magnified in beautifying them for us satisfies our self-love (*Centuries*, IV, 49).

If the universe appears as it really is, as it appears to the illuminated man, that is, supremely beautiful and supremely good, then there must follow a satisfaction of his natural desires so intense that there is an overflow of pleasure. Human nature in its finitude cannot take up this satisfaction in its entirety and it turns inevitably to the inexhaustible source of these pleasures as the only adequate object of love and rejoicing. The demands of the self are over-satisfied, as it were, and the superflux, demanding an object, looks beyond the self to its divine original: 'but when we do love ourselves, and self-love is satisfied infinitely in all its desires and possible demands, then it is easily led to regard the Benefactor more than itself, and for His sake overflows abundantly to all others. So that God by satisfying my self-love hath enacted and engaged me to love others'[1] (*Centuries*, IV, 55).

'Had we not loved ourselves at all, we could never have been obliged to love anything.' In this Traherne writes in complete agreement with the older medieval tradition of Cistercian mysticism. As we approach our full humanity through love so we become more fully the image of God which it is our essential nature to be, and in realizing our true nature lies Felicity: 'The more you love men, the more delightful you will be to God, and the more delights you will take in God and the more you will enjoy Him. So that the more like you are to Him in goodness, the more abundantly you will enjoy His goodness. By loving others you live in others to receive it' (*Centuries*, IV, 57). The delight is in the giving and the giving yields still more delight. There can be no excess of love for Traherne: 'It seems it will break in everywhere, as that without which the world could not be enjoyed' (*Centuries*, IV, 61). But how does St Bernard answer the question of the nature of the relation between the love of self and the love of God the fundamental kinship of which he affirms?

> . . . let him remove from his soul the iniquity which forms in her a partial unlikeness to the word and then there shall be perfect unity of spirit, mutual vision, and reciprocal love: 'When that which is perfect shall come, that which is in part shall be done away' and then between God and the soul shall be pure and perfect love, they shall know each other fully, behold each other clearly, they shall be united to each other firmly, they shall live together inseparably, they shall be like each other absolutely. Then shall the soul know God even as she is known; then shall she love as she is loved; and over His Bride shall rejoice the Bridegroom, knowing and known, loving and beloved, Jesus Christ our Lord who is over all things, God blessed for ever.[2]

Traherne writes of the development of the self through love when its potential nature is made fully actual that 'now there is an infinite union between Him and us, He being infinitely delightful, to us and we to Him. For He infinitely delighteth to see creatures act upon such illustrious and eternal principles, in a manner so divine, heroic and most truly blessed' (*Centuries*, IV, 49); and finally, Love, which is God, is 'Your true self' by which you become 'Holy, wise and just towards all things, blessed in all things, the Bride of God, glorious before all, His offspring and first born, and so like Him, that being described one would think it He' (*Centuries*, IV, 67).

---

[1] See also *Centuries*, IV, 60.   [2] St Bernard, *In Cantica Canticorum*, 82, 8.

The reconciliation of the love of self with love of God in Cistercian mysticism rests in the conscious effort made by the individual self to perfect

> a natural likeness of the soul to God by means of a conformity ever more fully realized, between the human will and the divine will. To love God is, in a way, to make God love Himself in us, as He loves Himself in Himself. That is the true meaning of the mystic marriage: *Talis conformitas maritat animam verbo, cum cui videlicet similis est per naturam, similem niholominus se exhibet per voluntatem, diligens sicut dilecta est. Ergo si perfecte diligit, nupsit.*[1]

Since God is love, since love is the divine essence (this is implied also in Traherne's words that 'God is not a mixt and compounded Being, so that His love is one thing and Himself another') (*Centuries*, IV, 39), then the love which human persons experience is always a return towards God, a 'love for the very substance of love, the end beyond which no other end exists'.[2] This is the ground on which the self finds union with God. Love by which, in Traherne's words, a man attains himself, is also that by which he becomes a similitude of God. By becoming like God man fulfils the desire of his true nature. In the words of William of St Thierry[3] from his *Epistola ad fratres de Monte Dei 'Et haec est hominis perfectio, similitudo Dei'*: 'to be like to God, that is man's perfection . . . love must at all costs be preserved from corruption, since for love we were made, for love we live, and to become like to God who were made in God's image'.[4]

I do not suggest that Traherne consciously drew upon the doctrines of the great Abbot of Clairvaux, but that there is a substantial similarity between the affirmations of the seventeenth-century English divine and those of the twelfth-century French monk who marks the high ideal of medieval monasticism is, I maintain, a fact of some importance. Certainly it is true that these conceptions of love are central to Christian doctrine and it is therefore not to be wondered at that reaffirmations should be made at intervals however widely spaced. What is interesting is to find the traditions of medieval religious thought persisting well into the seventeenth century. One feels that Traherne and the earlier contemplatives are on common ground in writing of Christian love in this way. They share a common mode of experience.

---

[1] E. Gilson, *The Spirit of Medieval Philosophy*, p. 300. The Latin quotation is from St Bernard's *In Cantica Canticorum*, 83, 2–3.

[2] E. Gilson, op. cit., p. 301.

[3] A disciple of St Bernard.

[4] William de St Thierry, *Epistola ad fratres de Monte Dei*, II, 3, 16.

By contrast these same ideas are those which to the modern mind are the most difficult fully to accept. We are familiar to-day with the love of self, the love of country or state, and a score of other loves, but the idea, still less the experience, of a universe sustained by love is remote from the life of those

> Who fear the injustice of men less than the justice of God;
> Who fear the hand at the window, the fire in the thatch,
> the fist in the tavern, the push into the canal,
> Less than we fear the Love of God.[1]

A modern author in a book on English mysticism[2] comments that Traherne's notion of self-love as the basis of all love, even the love of God, is an indication simply that he 'is a psychologist as well as a rhapsodist'. It would have been perhaps more to the point to have remarked that Traherne was clearly familiar with, or had arrived at independently, conceptions of the nature of love which are not included in the meanings which are given to the word to-day. Traherne's words in this context are evidence not so much of his knowledge of human nature in the sense in which the word psychologist is here attributed to him, a knowledge, for instance, that people occasionally do what is morally approved of for what, on inspection, seems to be less praiseworthy motives; they are, rather, significant of his ruling conviction that God and man cannot be separated and that final causes are to be considered always in observing human activity. Traherne's comments would be that it is God-like to love, and it is God-like to live in and for an object other than yourself; but we are all creatures of God and therefore we do good to ourselves when we do good to others: 'The more we live in all, the more we live in one' (*Centuries*, II, 61). In other words it is an excessively narrow interpretation to call Traherne no more than a psychologist in this context (implying that this is somehow valuable) as if he were concerned only with the detached and unprejudiced observation of how men's minds work when they are involved in self-love or in the love of God. The idea that he is expressing is as much a part of traditional mystical doctrine as the results of his own perceptions. One should call him a good theologian before calling him a good psychologist. This is not at all to detract from the value of his psychology, in the modern isolated sense, when he writes that the self must first be satisfied before love to others is

---

[1] T. S. Eliot, *Murder in the Cathedral* (London, 1935), p. 85.
[2] G. Bullett, *The English Mystics* (London, 1950), p. 111.

possible and that love to one's fellow men cannot be based on the hatred or the suppression of one's self. Harmony within the individual as a prime necessity before any useful social activity is likely is an idea of which modern psychologists would approve. But we must keep a proper perspective. Traherne would not have allowed that anything is entirely 'within' the individual. Where love exists God is present also, a more than human reality, which exists as 'your true self' as well as being 'of Himself', withdrawn from all creatures, pure love in the abstract, as Traherne phrases it. We participate in God even in loving ourselves. We may move towards God by losing our sense of self or move away from God by keeping our self-love 'self ended'. In either case we cannot escape from God. These are some of the implications of Traherne's mystical thought here, and any statement about his ability as a psychologist should surely take them into account.

A similar instance of an over-simplification which gives rise to a judgement which I suggest is shallow and misleading occurs in another work of recent years. D. Bush in *English Literature in the Earlier 17th Century* complains[1] of a certain 'inhumanity' in Traherne and of the presence of 'a large element of facile, expansive, emotional optimism, the kind of optimism which in the next generations passed easily into deistic sentimentalism'. Now a facile and sentimental optimism is based surely on ignorance and insensitivity, on a refusal to contemplate all aspects of a problem. It is the result of a partial response to a situation which produces an unwarranted cheerfulness, more wishful than intelligent. The facile optimist regarding himself and the world with equanimity hopes for the best without examining what the best may be and without taking positive action to bring about its realization. This criticism of Traherne's attitude and in particular of his conception of love is, I suggest, quite unjustified and one which reveals an unawareness of his essential mysticism. Traherne understands from his experience that perfection belongs only to the divine and that it is not to be found on the plane of human things except at the moment of illumination. At this moment he is indeed not human in the normal sense. He realizes perfection, an absolute satisfaction; he is 'all Act as God is'. After this union the two planes may well fall apart. The normal man resumes, though indeed after such knowledge he can never again be quite normal. One result of this experience is the knowledge that the supreme satisfaction is not to be found on an exclusively human level. God and only God is the source of satisfaction: 'We must love

[1] Oxford, 1945, p. 149.

them (*sc.* created things) infinitely, but in God, and for God; and God in them' (*Centuries*, II, 66). The purely human, in the everyday sense of the word, disappears, is integrated in the more than human reality. One admits the 'inhumanity'; Traherne's felicity lies in his sense of union with other modes of being and with the deity who is impersonal, who includes and surpasses the merely personal.

Traherne might well be accused of a facile optimism if he maintains that there is nothing wrong with man or his world, that nothing needs to be altered. But this is not so; the need for self-amendment, for a re-creation of purity is always affirmed by him as the necessary condition for the vision of this world as 'far better than Paradise'. The amendment of the self involves a radical change, a descent into 'the abyss of humility'. It is only when this change has taken place that Traherne can then say 'Thus you see I can make merry with calamities, and while I grieve at Sins, and war against them, abhorring the world, and myself more, descend into the abyss of humility, and there admire a new offspring and torrent of joys—God's Mercies' (*Centuries*, III, 38). The linking of calamities and God's Mercies is repeated finely in the *Fourth Century*: 'The sharpest trials are the finest furbishing. The most tempestuous weather is the best seed-time. A Christian is an oak flourishing in winter' (*Centuries*, IV, 91).

Traherne does not gloss over the state of mankind in a sentimental minimizing of the fact of evil:

> On every side we are environed with enemies, surrounded with reproaches, encompassed with wrongs, besieged with offences, receiving evil for good, being disturbed by fools, and invaded with malice. This is the true estate of the world, which lying in wickedness, as our Saviour witnesseth, yieldeth no better fruits, than the bitter clusters of folly and perverseness, the grapes of Sodom, and the seeds of Gomorrah. Blind wretches that wound themselves offend me. I need therefore the oil of pity and the balm of love to remedy and heal them. Did they see the beauty of Holiness or the face of Happiness they would not do so (*Centuries*, IV, 20).

There is no easy optimism here. The transforming and redeeming knowledge of the beauty of Holiness and the face of Happiness is not the self persuasion of sentiment; the words have the authority of proved facts. They have an objectivity, a truth to experience of the same kind as Traherne's other phrase of love: 'It seems it will break in everywhere, as that without which the world could not be enjoyed' (*Centuries*, IV, 61). This is not expansive nor indeed particularly emotional. It is a statement of what Traherne knows to be true. Elsewhere

Traherne writes: 'This estate wherein I am placed is the best for me; tho' encompassed with difficulties. It is my duty to think so, and I cannot do otherwise' (*Centuries*, IV, 89). Again taken in their context these words far from expressing a Panglossian complacency represent the insight of the mystic who has reached a point of awareness when good and evil are accepted positively as part of a divine pattern. What is there of deistic sentimentalism in these words: 'All sorrows should appear but shadows, besides that of His absence, and all the greatness of riches and estates swallowed up in the light of His favour' (*Centuries*, IV, 91)? The experience of the absence of God or of the nothingness of worldly success in comparison with His presence has little in common with eighteenth-century deism. Traherne's work is at once more complex and more profound than these two criticisms allow.

It is above all in his analysis of Christian love based on his own mystical experience as well as his doctrinal knowledge that he conveys a sense of the complexity of what is also a fundamentally unifying experience. This is seen most clearly in what he writes of the relation of love to the conception of the Trinity. Love is a unifying power which yet upholds the individuality of the members which are included in a more than personal whole. Love to Traherne is a constant and creative activity: it is also the medium which must be present for the activity to be possible at all. It is the sea and the wave in the sea. Traherne sees in love the mystery of the Trinity:

> In all love there is a love begetting, and a love begotten, and a love proceeding. Which though they are one in essence subsist nevertheless in three several manners. For love is benevolent affection to another. Which is of itself and by itself related to its object. It floweth from itself and resteth in its object. Love proceedeth of necessity from itself, *for unless it be of itself it is not love.*[1] Constraint is destructive and opposite to its nature. The love from which it floweth is the fountain of love. The love which streameth from it, is the communication of love, or love communicated. The love which resteth in the object is the love which streameth to it. So that in all love, the Trinity is clear. By secret passages without stirring it proceedeth to its object and is as powerfully present as if it did not proceed at all. The love that lieth in the bosom of the Lover being the love that is perceived in the spirit of the Beloved: that is, the same in substance, tho' in the manner of substance, or subsistence, different. Love in the stream is the effect of Love, Love seen, or dwelling in the object proceedeth from both. Yet are all these, one and the selfsame Love: though three Loves (*Centuries*, II, 40).

---

[1] My italics.

If Love is always the 'one and the self-same Love' then God is present where love is present. Love is then the giving of God to the object of His Love; the object that is loved is inevitably a part of the cause of all Love. Here again is an idea which is completely in the spirit of medieval Christian theology: 'Cistercian mysticism is altogether suspended from a theology of the Trinity of which the central idea would seem to be that God Himself lives by a law, and that the law that rules His intimate life is love. The Father generates the Son, and the bond that unites the Son to the Father and the Father to the Son is the Spirit Who is their mutual love.'[1] Love is the bond which assures the unity of the divine life. This is a summary by an acknowledged authority of a key position on the medieval doctrine. Traherne's thought is strikingly similar. In all Love 'The Trinity is clear'; 'Where Love is the Lover, Love streaming from the Lover, is the Lover;[2] the Lover streaming from himself, and existing in another Person' (*Centuries*, II, 42). 'This Person is the Son of God: who as He is the Wisdom of the Father, so is He the Love of the Father. For the Love of the Father is the Wisdom of the Father. And this Person did God by loving us, beget, that He might be the means of all our glory' (*Centuries*, II, 43).

Traherne proceeds to make a closer analysis of love in its threefold nature which is a replica of the Trinity, which indeed, in the profoundest sense, is the Trinity:

> In all Love there is some Producer, some Means and some End; all these being internal in the thing itself. Love loving is the Producer, and that is the Father; Love produced is the Means, and that is the Son. For Love is the means by which a lover loveth. The end of these means is Love for it is love by loving and that is the Holy Ghost. The end and the Producer being both the same, by the Means attained. For by loving Love attaineth itself and being. The Producer is attained by loving, and is the End of Himself. That Love is the end of itself and that God loveth that He might be love, is as evident to him that considers spiritual things as the Sun (*Centuries*, II, 46).

Traherne makes these distinctions between love the producer, love the means, and love the end quite firmly and confidently. This might be accounted for by a close acquaintance with the medieval tradition and a study of the theology of the Trinity. Alternatively he may have arrived at these distinctions in the effort of giving a faithful account of

[1] E. Gilson, op. cit., p. 298.
[2] Cf. the relation of the 'flame to its light' of patristic theology: 'Think of fire as a father, light as a son'. St Augustine, *Sermo ad Catechumenos*, section 8.

his own experience of mystical love. Both alternatives may well be true. In either case the difficulty of what he writes is the same; and it is the same kind of difficulty as that with which we are confronted in contemplating the dogma of the Trinity. It is a mystery, to be grasped fully by experience only. Apart from the analogy with the Trinity this passage can convey a more general impression of the nature of love. For instance, Traherne writes that the end and the producer are identified, and this identity is 'by the Means attained', by love. This threefold distinction is internal in the unity which is the whole experience of love. One response to this is to apprehend love as a self-creating activity, a continuous dynamic process. It is not a static condition but an endless flow of energy through a circuit. It is an essentially mutual activity, a movement to and from two elements, a circulation. At the same time it is a unity.

I think this passage does nothing to remove the mystery at the heart of this conception. It does reflect, however, a mode of experience. Traherne is aware of love as indivisible, as self-complete, and yet it is also a relationship in which a trinary structure is discernible. Each act of love is complete, has its own individuality. Within each act the relationship occurs of father and son, producer and that which is produced, subject and object. Each creates and is created by the other. The one cannot exist without the other. This mutuality is itself the third element in this structure; each individual act of love involves the universal love which sustains creation. As a deduction from this, one may say that to have a profound experience of unity an equally profound perception of the distinctions involved is necessary. The distinctions go to make the experience of unity. And this is certainly true of Traherne's general position. It is characteristic of the man that this analysis which is in form and content akin to medieval scholasticism should end with an appeal to experience. Indeed, we must suppose that Traherne is using the terms traditional to Christian thought because they are those which in a time of change and conflict are still for him the most adequate for the expression of his religious experience. This meditation on the nature of love achieves its climax:

> Love is the Spirit of God. In Himself it is the Father, or else the Son, for the Father is in the Son, and the Son is in the Father: In us it is the Holy Ghost. The love of God being seen, being God in us: Purifying, illuminating, strengthening, and comforting the soul of the seer. For God by shewing communicated Himself to men and angels. And when He dwelleth in the soul, dwelleth in the sight. And when He dwelleth in the sight achieving all

that love can do for such a soul. For this the world serveth you as it is a mirror wherein you contemplate the Blessed Trinity. For it plainly sheweth that God is Love, and in His being Love you see the unity of the Blessed Trinity, and a glorious Trinity in the Blessed Unity (*Centuries*, II, 45).

The world can mirror the divine love—and this is a crucial point— because a redeemer has been prepared for us to refine our nature and 'to purge out the poison and the filthy plague of Sin' (*Centuries*, II, 45). As I have pointed out in an earlier chapter,[1] the fact that man and nature have been redeemed by Christ's sacrifice is a consistent condition of Traherne's thought. It is indeed Love which has been the means of this cosmic purification, the love which is Christ as well as the Father. Man and nature have been redeemed and therefore there is no reason in the nature of things why the state of innocence should not be regained. The burden of choice is put on man. If he so wishes, if he will see again with the eyes of the child, then the experience of the world as Paradise can be enjoyed as man's inheritance here and now. It is Traherne's vision that through the love which is the very law of God's being the perfect world of Eden now 'lost and buried in ruins, nothing appearing but fragments . . . worthless shreds and parcels' (*Centuries*, IV, 54) can be restored, and this life become again the 'mirror wherein you contemplate the Blessed Trinity'.

Finally we see that because of this very law of love the fully realized individual cannot exist in isolation, as a self-sufficient being. Whenever Traherne speaks of himself as being sole heir of the Universe he invariably speaks at the same time of all other persons as being so likewise. We become truly ourselves when we become fully aware of the life of other individuals. The individual attains himself in ceasing to be merely individual. Love seeks always an object other than itself in which to live nor is it satisfied with any finite object: 'God alone cannot be beloved. He cannot be loved with a finite love, because He is infinite. Were he beloved alone His love would be limited. He must be loved in all with an unlimited love, even in all His doings, in all His friends, in all His creatures. Everywhere in all things thou must meet His love and this the law of Nature commands' (*Centuries*, I, 72). It is when we have renounced our finite love, our preoccupation with 'I', 'me' and 'mine', that we can truly possess our inheritance. We are the heirs of the world, but Traherne's meaning is surely that all things are ours provided that we regard nothing as exclusively ours. We must enjoy the world as in God and for God:

[1] Chapter III.

He giveth all the world to me, He giveth it to everyone in giving it to all, and giveth it wholly to me in giving it to everyone for every one's sake. . . . Here is love! Here is a Kingdom! Where all are knit in infinite unity. All are happy in each other. All are like Deities. Every one the end of all things, every one supreme, every one a treasure and the joy of all, and every one most infinitely delighted in being so (*Centuries*, I, 74).

By love we are united with God and with our fellow men: 'By love our Souls are married and solder'd to the creatures: and it is our Duty like God to be united to them all. We must love them infinitely but in God, and for God; and God in them:' (*Centuries*, II, 66). The universe is not empty or meaningless; it can only appear so to the man who is without full knowledge of his own true nature. And this is to be a similitude of God, to actualize our potential being. When this is achieved then all things become significant of God's purpose. To the mystic nothing is without meaning. This is the ground for Traherne's exultation. Like God he can see in a river, a drop of water, an apple, a grain of sand or corn

infinite excellencies. . . . He seeth how it relateth to angels and men: how it proceedeth from the most perfect Lover to the most perfectly Beloved; How it representeth all His attributes; how it conduceth in its place, by the best of means to the best of ends; and for this cause it cannot be beloved too much. God the Author and God the End is to be beloved in it. . . . O what a treasure is every sand when truly understood! Who can love anything that God made too much? What a world would this be, were everything beloved as it ought to be! (*Centuries*, II, 67).

This is Traherne's vision, this is his experience of what to him is the truth. This vision belongs still to the world which T. S. Eliot calls the world of the *high dream*.[1] It involves a renunciation of the simply personal self and this is a practice alien to the modern world. Traherne stands at the very end of a period when this vision was recognized and accepted as central to Christian experience. In the new world which was growing during the century in which Traherne lived and wrote, and which is our world to-day, these experiences are relegated to the sphere of the eccentric, or in the pejorative modern sense, of the merely visionary. In his vision love is indeed the great hierophant by which that which is finite becomes more than itself:

Infinite Love cannot be expressed in finite room: but must have infinite places wherein to utter and shew itself. It must therefore fill all Eternity and

---

[1] T. S. Eliot, *Selected Essays*, p. 262.

the Omnipresence of God with joys and treasures for my fruition. And yet it must be expressed in a private room by making me able in a centre to enjoy them. It must be infinitely exprest in the smallest moment by making me in every moment to see them all. It is both ways infinite, for my Soul is an infinite sphere in a centre. By this way you know that you are infinitely beloved: God hath made your spirit a centre in eternity comprehending all, and filled all about you in an endless manner with infinite riches: which shine before you and surround you with divine and Heavenly enjoyments (*Centuries*, II, 80).

Through concentration on what appears finite and limited, by full enjoyment of the sensible world we may approach the infinite. But Traherne in his flashes of illumination sees nothing as simply finite. Both nature and humanity are capable of infinity and perpetually point towards it: 'infinite worth shut up in the limits of a material being, is the only way to a real infinity' (*Centuries*, III, 20). It is the infinite possibilities of man and nature that Traherne habitually stresses rather than their limitations. There is nothing in Traherne of the doubt and agony of spirit in which Donne or Hopkins seeks the love of God. The sense of human life as tragic is absent from Traherne's mind. In his unbounded confidence and assurance he looks forward to the vision of Blake's world in which 'If the doors of perception were cleansed, everything would appear as it is, infinite'.[1]

[1] W. Blake, *Works*, ed. cit., 'The Prophetic Books', p. 185.

CHAPTER VII

The Imagery of Traherne

THERE is what seems to be an anticipation of Coleridge in the opening sections of the first book of the *Centuries*: 'I will utter Things that have been kept secret from the foundation of the World. Things Strange yet Common; Incredible, yet Known; Most High, yet plain; infinitely Profitable, but not Esteemed' (*Centuries*, I, iii). The idea of reconciling things 'Strange yet Common; Incredible yet Known' is part of Coleridge's theory of the power and function of the Imagination (*B.L.*, chap. XIV), and 'the Soul that is everywhere, and in each' (*B.L.*, chap. XIII), which to Coleridge is Imagination, is also the centre of Traherne's meditations and of his enjoyment. The resemblance springs from the powerful impulse in both men to see their world as a unity. Traherne, though, is not concerned with defining a theory of poetry but with expressing a way of life, to piece 'this life with the life of Heaven, and seeing it as one with all Eternity, a Part of it, a Life within it' (*Centuries*, IV, 93). His practice as a poet springs directly from ecstatic experience, and the nature of his mysticism determines the quality of his poetry.

Such a relation is by no means inevitable; indeed mysticism and poetry are, in certain respects, antagonistic. The poet is above all concerned with words and their order; his medium is words and the essential 'meaning' of the poem is not separable from the words of the poem, words as spoken, and in their unique arrangement. Coleridge is profoundly right when he proposes the test of the 'blameless style' as its '*untranslateableness* in words of the same language without injury to the meaning' (*B.L.*, chap. XXII). The 'meaning' of, for instance, Marvell's 'Lines to his Coy Mistress' is not to be identified with the experiences of love-making or with our anxieties over the passing of time; these are constituents, certainly, but the experience, which is the poem, would not have existed had not the poem been written. A good poem is, quite literally, a new experience, not simply the communication of a state of mind once enjoyed or suffered by the poet to which the poem takes us back. The best poetry of Wordsworth, one of the most reminiscent of all poets, does not depend on our sympathy with the poet's emotions as they were prior to the writing of the poem, but lives with a life of its own, creates a new meaning from the body of feelings, memories and reflections of which it has been made. I would claim this to be true of poems as different as 'A Slumber did my Spirit seal' and *Michael*.

The poet's primary concern with language and all its possible effects separates him from the mystic, the pure mystic, the author, for instance, of *The Cloud of Unknowing*.[1] In this work the experience at its centre is ineffable, and the author is not attempting the impossible task of communicating this experience, that of union with the divine ground of being, incomprehensible and without attributes. To do so he would have to use images, forms and words which would modify, limit and distort the purity of this experience. What he is doing is expressed in Eliot's lines, 'I can only say, *there* we have been: but I cannot say where. And I cannot say, how long, for that is to place it in time' (*Burnt Norton*).

The Cloud of Unknowing, which is the finest work of mystical writing in fourteenth-century England and perhaps in the whole of our literature, does not seek to convey in other terms what it is like to enjoy mystical experience but rather to set down the conditions under which this may come about. These conditions require that we must 'forget alle the creatures that ever God made and the works of them, so that thy thought ne thy desire be not directe to any of them, neither in general ne in special. But let them be and take no kepe to them.'[2] The world of the senses is not to be trusted; God is unknowable through his works nor is the understanding capable of comprehending God; we can 'never by the work of . . . understanding come to the knowing of an unmade goostely thing, the whiche is nothing else but only God. And therefore it was that Seynte Denis seyde: "the moste goodly knowyng of God is that, the which is knowyn by unknowyng"' (*The Cloud*, p. 125).

To come to the stage where this 'knowledge' may be possible the contemplative must not only empty his mind of images and desires attaching to material and physical objects but of all images and thoughts of God; both image and thought must die away: 'And loke that nothing leve in thy working mind but a naked entent streching into God, not clothed in any specyal thought of God in hymself, how he is in him-self or in any of his werkes but only that he is as he is' (*The

---

[1] *The Cloud of Unknowing*, ed. Hodgson (London, 1944).
[2] *The Cloud*, p. 16.

Book of Privy Counselling, ed. Hodgson, p. 135). When this clearing away of all images from the mind is achieved a final obstacle remains, the sense of self as an individual, separate being. This also must disappear if the supreme mystical experience is to be enjoyed. This final clearing away of distractions can only take place, the author of *The Cloud* affirms, by the special grace of God.

This brief account of the teaching of *The Cloud of Unknowing* may serve to show the conflict that can occur between the activity of the poet and the highest experiences of the mystic. The poet lives in a world of sensible forms; he must use verbal forms; they make him what he is. Whereas the mystic in the tradition of *The Cloud*, and it is part of a tradition, is seeking always to get free from the world of forms. He must enter into a state of intellectual deprivation and imaginative emptiness.

If this is the highest or most pure form of mysticism, then it cannot be expressed in words, whether in poetry or prose; it can only be alluded to: 'I can only say, *there* we have been.' It would be quite unjustified to place Traherne as a mystic together with the author of *The Cloud*, but nevertheless the nature of Traherne's mysticism is sufficiently advanced to affect the use of images and metaphors in his poetry. In brief, the distinctive quality of Traherne's poetry lies in its double awareness, an awareness of the world of the senses and of the spirit as equally delightful. Metaphors drawn from the pleasures of taste are used not only to express the human delight in the very fact of living but that of the bodiless angels who

> . . . have neither ears nor eyes,
> Nor tongues nor hands,
> Yet feel the Delights of all the World,
> And hear the Harmonies, not only which
> Earth but Heaven maketh.
> (*Thanksgivings for the Body*, ll. 405-9)[1]

In his imagery Traherne writes of the senses as if they were spiritual and of the spirit as if it were sensuous. The taste of 'Honey, Milk and Butter' (*Thanksgivings for the Body*, l. 403) expresses both natural and supernatural enjoyments.

Yet Traherne is a mystic before he is a poet. He is not involved in 'the intolerable wrestle with words and meanings' or with the excitement of discovering what he thinks and feels in the very process of

[1] Traherne, *Centuries, Poems, and Thanksgivings*, vol. II, ed. Margoliouth (Oxford, 1958), p. 225.

creating a poem. He does not, like Donne, seek to tame an emotion by
fettering it in verse. He is not, that is, primarily interested in words;
he has his ecstatic vision of the world. This vision exists whether or not
a poem comes into being. The poetry is important as the vehicle for
conveying to us Traherne's sense of vital enjoyment, and the less the
words get in the way the better they serve this end. This is the ground
for his declaration in favour of simplicity in writing:

> On Shining Banks we could nigh *Tagus* walk;
> In flow'ry Meads of rich *Pactolus* talk:
> Bring in the *Druids*, and the *Sybills* view;
> See what the Rites are which the *Indians* do;
> Derive along the channel of our Quill
> The streams that flow from high *Parnassus* hill;
> Ransack all Nature's Rooms, and add the things
> Which *Persian* Courts enrich; to make Us Kings:
> To make us Kings indeed! Not verbal Ones,
> But real Kings, exalted unto Thrones;
> And more than Golden Thrones! 'Tis this I do,
> Letting Poëtick Strains and Shadows go.
>
> . . . .
>
> Ev'n thus do idle Fancies, Toys, and Words
> (Like gilded Scabbards hiding rusty Swords)
> Take vulgar Souls; who gaze on rich Attire
> But God's diviner Works do ne'r admire.
>   (*The Author to the Critical Peruser*)[1]

Traherne, like Herbert in his Jordan poems, claims that truth can
best be seen when 'curling Metaphors', 'florid streams of superficial
Gems', '*Zamzummim* words' and 'tongues that sound like *Babel-Hell*'
are quietly discarded. This claim springs from his beliefs:

> The Naked Things
> Are most Sublime, and Brightest shew,
>   When they alone are seen:
> Mens Hands then Angels wings
> Are truer wealth even here below:
>   For those but seem.
> Their Worth they then do best reveal,
> When we all Metaphores remove,
>   For Metaphores conceal,
>   And only Vapours prove.
>   (*The Person*, ll. 17–26)

---

[1] Op. cit., vol. II, p. 2.

These words do, in fact, reflect Traherne's practice in using images. There is a relative infrequency of overt metaphor, as one might expect, and also, if we compare him with Herbert, a lack of imaginative solidity in his poetry.

In Herbert's *The Quip* we are aware of a world of actuality:

> First, Beautie crept into a rose
> Which when I pluckt not, Sir, said she,
> Tell me, I pray, Whose hands are those?
> *But thou shalt answer, Lord, for me.*

> Then Money came, and chinking still,
> What tune is this, poore man? saith he:
> I heard in Musick you had skill.
> *But thou shalt answer, Lord, for me.*

> Then came brave Glorie puffing by
> In silks that whistled, who but he?
> He scarce allow'd me half an eie.
> *But thou shalt answer, Lord, for me.*

Here is a dramatic immediacy; we are conscious of the presence of the speaking voice in the rhythms and tone of the verse: 'What tune is this, poore man?' Hardly ever do we find in Traherne's poetry a comparable sense of actual, concrete life; 'In silks that whistled, who but he?' By contrast there is a thinness in Traherne's imagery, an absence of dramatic enactment of his feelings. His ecstasy overshadows his images. We are given, instead, a list of items, of words serving as pointers. Indeed, words seem inadequate for Traherne to express his vision; but if metaphors are felt to be 'vapours' only, veils of the truth, then this is what we would expect.

> No Gold, nor Trade, nor Silver there,
> Nor Cloaths, no Coin, nor Houses were,
> No gaudy Coaches, Feasts, or Palaces,
> Nor vain Inventions newly made to pleas;
> But native Truth, and Virgin-Purity,
> An uncorrupt simplicity.
> (*Adam*, ll. 13–18)

This is statement, dramatically inert. Traherne is telling us what he sees, and what he sees is, for him, bathed in so brilliant a light that he does not distinguish or particularize. Herbert, by contrast, is presenting, through the rhythms and tone of his words, a particular scene or episode. It is significant that Traherne is relatively fond of comparisons with metals and jewels, shining dazzling things. 'Burnisht' is a frequent word (*The Salutation*, l. 19, *Speed*, l. 25); 'orient pearls', 'golden streams' (*Silence*, l. 72); 'golden stones' (*Wonder*, l. 33); 'Rich Diamond and Pearl and Gold' (*Wonder*, l. 41); these are his characteristic terms of praise for the world, in his ecstatic vision.

What I have described as a lack of imaginative solidity in Traherne's imagery and the related weakness in the dramatic quality of his poetry may be described as a poetic failure; it is certainly a consequence of his mystical vision and it reflects the problem of the mystic in expressing his experiences at all. In a sense Traherne is not profoundly interested in objects as objects, and for the poet this is a disadvantage, since words are objects for him. There is a key line in *The Preparative* which goes to the heart of this issue:

> 'Tis not the Object, but the Light
> That maketh Heaven; 'Tis Purer sight.
> Felicitie
> Appears to none but them that purely see.
> (ll. 57–60)

The world of sensible objects to Traherne becomes his possession; it is included within himself:

> The World was more in me, than I in it.
> (*Silence*, l. 81)

> An Object, if it were before
> My Ey, was by Dame Natures Law,
> Within my Soul. Her store
> Was all at once within me.
> (*My Spirit*, ll. 37–40)

This is Traherne's most deeply felt experience, that he is the heir of all creation, and his most remarkable use of words centres in this, in the 'deep Abysses of Delight' (*The Approach*, l. 35) he feels within him. If all outward objects are able to be absorbed within his consciousness, then it is not surprising that there is an absence of specific distinction in his expression of enjoyment of particular objects. All things, all images are equally wonderful to the purified mind:

> Proprieties themselves were mine,
> And Hedges Ornaments;
> Walls, Boxes, Coffers, and their rich contents
> Did not Divide my Joys, but shine.

> Clothes, Ribbons, Jewels, Laces, I esteemed
>   My Joys by others worn;
> For me they all to wear them seemd
>   When I was born.
>
> (*Wonder*, ll. 57–64)

This is the characteristic listing of objects, all to be delighted in with equal intensity because part of the infinite whole. The effect, though, as poetry, is often that of a rhapsodic monotone, for instance, the final stanza of *My Spirit*:

> O Wondrous Self! O sphere of Light,
> O sphere of Joy most fair;
> O Act, O Power infinit;
> O Subtile, and unbounded Air!
>   O Living Orb of Sight!
> Thou which within me art, yet Me! Thou Ey,
> And Temple of his Whole Infinitie!

If the world of creation can be felt to be contained within the self, then the self must be felt as infinite, and it is the effort to express this miraculous sensation that yields Traherne's most remarkable verse. He marvels at the very fact of the human body, his 'azure veins'—the adjective calls up the sky and its infinity as well as the brilliance of heraldic colour—the 'Lims in Boys' are 'Sacred Treasures' (*The Salutation*, l. 21).

> A Native Health and Innocence
>   Within my Bones did grow
> And while my GOD did all his Glories shew,
>   I felt a Vigour in my Sence
> That was all SPIRIT. I within did flow
>   With Seas of Life, like Wine;
> I nothing in the World did know,
>   But 'twas Divine.
>
> (*Wonder*, ll. 17–24)

This image of the 'Seas of Life' flowing in his veins 'like wine' is a fine achievement; it appears in a different and even finer form in *The Centuries*: 'You never enjoy the world aright, till the Sea itself floweth in your veins' (I, 29), a more dramatic, vigorous and more deeply metaphorical expression than in the poem; his best poetry is often to be found in his prose.

'Within my Bones', the 'abysses of delight'—Traherne is seeking to convey his conviction that the infinity of pleasure which is everywhere in creation is also at the very centre of his being. He is attempting imaginatively to express a logical contradiction; he does so by a statement 'My Essence was Capacitie' (*My Spirit*, l. 8), but this statement is itself part of a metaphor, that the self is a sphere or hollow orb:

> A Strange Extended Orb of Joy
>   Proceeding from within
> Which did on evry side convey
> Itself, and being nigh of Kin
>   To God did evry way
> Dilate it self even in an Instant, and
> Like an Indivisible Centre Stand
> At once Surrounding all Eternitie.
>   (*My Spirit*, ll. 86–93)

The attempt to express the inexpressible leads him almost to the twentieth-century astronomer's phrase 'finite but unbounded'. T. S. Eliot, a greater poet than Traherne, recognizes what his art cannot do in the words from *Burnt Norton* I have already quoted: 'I can only say, *there* we have been: but I cannot say where. And I cannot say, how long, for that is to place it in time.' Eliot's lines express, by their very negation, a sense of mystery more effectively than any use of the word 'strange' or 'mysterious'; at the same time he knows what is possible to his art in the use of verbal economy and vivid particular instances to suggest the paradox of the infinite and the finite, and eternity in the instant:

> Here, the intersection of the timeless moment
> Is England and nowhere. Never and always.

> _____

> So, while the light fails
> On a winter's afternoon, in a secluded chapel
> History is now and England.
>   (*Little Gidding*)

By this standard Traherne is verbose, even clumsy; but he does attempt a first-hand description, and if he tries to say too much it is because, unlike Eliot, he is carried away by an enthusiasm to proclaim to his reader that we can all share this ecstasy (that he describes it as 'instantaneous dilation' is an irrelevance), that we are all possible heirs of the world. The extraordinary fact about Traherne's mode of writing is precisely this infusion of sustained and excited exhilaration; his eyes are 'living stars', 'I within did flow with Seas of Life':

> The Moon and Stars, the Air and Sun
>   Into my Chamber com:
> The Seas and Rivers hither flow,
> Yea, here the Trees of *Eden* grow
>   The Fowls and Fishes stand,
>   Kings and their Thrones,
> As 'twere, at my Command;
> God's Wealth, His Holy Ones,
> The Ages too, and Angels all conspire:
> While I, that I the Center am, admire.
>   (*Hosanna*, ll. 15–24)

This is Traherne at his most characteristic, and at his best, in poetry; all creation, all places, powers and times are present in his chamber, and his chamber is himself. Yet, as poetry, it lacks the concentration of Donne's

> She is all States, and all Princes, I,
> Nothing else is.

> ———————————

> Shine here to us, and thou art everywhere;
> This bed thy center is, these walls, thy sphere.
>   (*The Sunne Rising*)

Traherne's poetry does not so much present an experience as point to what the author sees and knows; if we are not already in some respect sympathetic to his vision on other grounds, the poetry will not make us intimately share in it. We are impressed not by the wonder of the universe as Traherne sees it but with wonder that he sees it as he does, with the thought how wonderful to be able to experience life in this way. The poetry is less fine than the experience.

His prose can offer more than the poetry; there are moments when the intensity and enthusiasm of the man's vision is matched by an equal strength of sound, rhythm and sensitivity in the words:

> The Corn was Orient and Immortal wheat, which never should be reaped, nor was ever sown. I thought it had stood from everlasting to everlasting. The Dust and Stones of the Street were as Precious as Gold. The Gates were at first the End of the World. The Green Trees when I saw them first through one of the Gates Transported and Ravished me: . . . Boys and Girles Tumbling in the Street, and Playing, were moving Jewels.

This is far more effective as communication of a sense of infinity than any catalogue of superlatives or reiterations of the word 'infinite'. Here is a dramatic, and rhythmic, particularity, 'Boys and Girles Tumbling in the Street, and Playing', a concentration on the local and vivid to evoke an actual sensory response in the reader which is often lacking in the poetry.

Coleridge's requirement of '*untranslateableness* in the words of the same language without injury to the meaning' is more than met in 'The Corn was Orient and Immortal wheat, which never should be reaped, nor was ever sown'. What this says cannot be distinguished from what it is, a unique order of words. Here is 'the balance and reconcilement' of opposites which Coleridge points to as the distinctive quality of the imagination manifesting itself in poetry; the 'reconcilement of sameness, with difference; of the general with the concrete; the idea with the image; the individual with the representative; the sense of novelty and freshness with old and familiar objects' (*B.L.*, chap. XIV). Nothing could seem simpler; the familiar words 'corn' and 'wheat' balanced with the unusual 'orient' and 'immortal' yet the result is a great imaginative achievement, a sense of the infinite conveyed through concentration on finite detail.

These moments of greatness in expression are, admittedly, rare in Traherne's writings; a comparable passage to which I have frequently referred occurs in the *First Century* (29): 'You never enjoy the world aright till the Sea itself floweth in your veins, till you are clothed with the heavens, and crowned with the stars.' It is perhaps no accident that the only passage of prose in English that could be appropriately placed with this for its peculiar and thrilling imaginative impact was written by a man with the same delight in the world of senses and an equally intense religious vision, I mean D. H. Lawrence: 'We ought to dance with rapture that we should be alive and in the flesh, and part of the living, incarnate cosmos. I am part of the sun as my eye is part of me. That I am part of the earth my feet know perfectly, and my blood is part of the sea.'[1]

To enjoy the world aright we must feel ourselves part of a living universe, a 'vivid and nourishing relation', in Lawrence's words, and words and images in themselves are for Traherne insufficient to approach this consummation. The sea must flow in your veins, an act is needed, a way of life established: 'It is no use asking for a Word to fulfil such a need. No Word, no Logos, no Utterance will ever do it. . . . It is the

[1] *Apocalypse* (London, 1932), p. 223.

Deed of life we have now to learn (D. H. Lawrence, *À propos of Lady Chatterley's Lover*, pp. 81–2). Traherne's words, whether in prose or poetry, are not so much the agents or instruments of artistic creativity as exhortations to the learning of this deed.

CHAPTER VIII

Traherne and The 'De Diligendo Deo' of St Bernard of Clairvaux

THE meditations on Christian love which Traherne makes in the second and fourth *Centuries* bear a general resemblance to the doctrine expressed by St Bernard in the work *De Diligendo Deo* (c. 1126). It is not possible to say positively whether Traherne had first-hand knowledge of this work or whether he was following a tradition deriving from the teaching of St Bernard. The second possibility seems more likely. St Bernard sets out clearly four degrees of Christian love. Traherne is concerned mainly with the first two and does not follow him closely into the profundities of the third and fourth degrees. It would seem hardly likely that a man writing on Christian love in a work intended for spiritual guidance should not at least set out the whole conception of love as St Bernard has expressed it even though his personal experience may have extended only to the first degrees. St Bernard's treatise is of a unity so complex and yet so well knit that had Traherne studied it at first hand a closer resemblance to the form of the work as a whole could be expected. It looks as though Traherne is taking or remembering elements which were useful to him from a general body of traditional doctrine with which he was familiar, without specific differentiation.

St Bernard begins his work by affirming that God is the cause of all love; the reason for loving God is God himself and there is no limit to the love we owe God: '*Vultis ergo a me audire, quare et quomodo diligendus sit Deus? et ego: Causa diligendi Deum, Deus est; modus, sine modo diligere.*'[1] It is a most significant difference that Traherne puts his emphasis on the unlimited love we should give not only to God but also to the works of God. It is the sensible creation through which God is manifest that Traherne also adores: 'Never was anything in this World loved too much, but many things have been loved in a false way: and all in too short a measure' (*Centuries*, II, 66). 'Who can love

[1] St Bernard, *De Diligendo Deo, Opera Omnia (Patrologiae Latinae*, ed. J.-P. Migne, Paris, 1862, Tome CLXXXII), vol. I, chap. I, para. I, col. 974.

122

anything that God made too much? What a world would this be, were everything beloved as it ought to be?' (*Centuries*, II, 67). One does not find in Traherne the consistent distinctions which are vital to the more powerful intelligence of St Bernard.

St Bernard proceeds to examine the reasons why we are compelled to love God. We must do so because of our dependence on God. He is the source of that which is essential to bodily life, for instance, food, sunlight and air; He is the ground also of the higher qualities of man's nature. These are dignity, wisdom, and virtue. By dignity, St Bernard means free will; by wisdom, the power to recognize this dignity and to understand that it is not a human achievement; by virtue, the impulse to seek, and, when found, to hold fast to the source of human being: '*Dignitatem in homine liberum arbitrium dico: . . . Scientiam vero, qua eamdem in se dignitatem agnoscat, non a se tamen. Pono virtutem, qua subinde ipsum a quo est, et inquirat non segniter, et teneat fortiter cum invenerit.*'[1]

Each of these three qualities has a twofold character. Dignity is not only the distinctive human prerogative but the cause why man has power over the animal world. Wisdom recognizes this distinction but acknowledges that although in us it is not of us: '*Scientia quoque duplex erit, si hanc ipsum dignitatem, vel aliud quodque bonum in nobis, et nobis inesse, et a nobis non esse noverimus.*'[2] Virtue impels us to cling to God when we have found Him. Dignity without wisdom and wisdom without virtue are valueless. These three gifts are mutually dependent for their right action.

St Bernard lays emphasis on true humility, the recognition of human limitations. We must know what we are, admit our dependent nature. It is not of ourselves that we are what we are: '*Utrumque ergo scias necesse est, et quid sis, et quod a te ipso non sis: ne aut omnino videlicet non glorieris, aut inaniter glorieris.*'[3] But man must also know what he is capable of; we must guard against ranking ourselves too low. We are distinguished from the rest of the animals by the possession of reason and we must recognize this. There are thus two kinds of ignorance both consisting in an incomplete realization of our nature. The worse kind is that which usurps the glory which is due to God alone. All good proceeds from God, and we are guilty of pride if we see the good as a rightful attribute of human nature; it is the gift of God alone. We are as stewards of what is excellent: '*est quippe superbia et delictum*

---

[1] St Bernard, op. cit., chap. II, para. 2, col. 976.
[2] Ibid., para. 3, col. 976.   [3] Ibid., para. 4, col. 976.

maximum, uti datis tanquam innatis; et in acceptis beneficiis gloriam usurpare beneficii'.[1]

All things depend from God. This is a law of nature. Therefore even the unbeliever, the man who has no knowledge of Christianity must realize this dependence if he knows himself. Man's own innate justice and common sense cry out from within that he is bound to love the very source from which he derives all things: *'Proinde inexcusabilis est omnis etiam infidelis, si non diligit Dominum Deum suum ex toto corde, tota anima, tota virtute sua. Clamat nempe intus ei innata, et non ignorata rationi justitia, quia ex toto se illum diligere debeat, cui, se totum debere non ignorat.'*[2]

Although we are moved to love God because of his manifest benefits to us, nevertheless the highest love we can give to God is to love Him for his own sake. This is fundamental in St Bernard's doctrine. God is not to be loved on account of any consequences which may be to our advantage. The man who loves God truly asks no other reward than God Himself; this love is spontaneous and impulsive. God is to be loved because He is God: *'Verus amor seipso contentus est. Habet praemium, sed id quod amatur.'*[3]

It is natural for men to be discontented with what they already possess and to seek to enlarge their property, to gain higher office or increased power. But nowhere is there final satisfaction to be gained from such things because the best is not to be found on this level; yet it is natural that man should continue to seek until he finds the best. It is his nature to be content only with the highest: *'Et quid mirum si inferioribus et deterioribus contentus non sit, qui citra summum vel optimum quiescere non potest?'*[4] Man's error lies in seeking the highest where it does not exist. Man will not find his satisfaction in the things of this world; peace is with God alone: *'Porro ibi quiesceret: quia sicut citra nulla revocat quies; sic nulla ultra jam inquietudo sollicitat.'*[5] We do not find in Traherne this sense of rest and stillness which God alone can give. His emphasis is on enjoyment and he can find his satisfaction through the world of nature, in the stars and the sky. Traherne's discontent is not with creatures but with the artifices of human society. St Bernard can find ultimate satisfaction in the creator alone. He seeks the God who is the efficient cause as well as the final end of our love. These are, also, words that Traherne echoes constantly: *'Causa diligendi*

---

[1] St. Bernard, op. cit., chap. II, para. 4, col. 977.
[2] Ibid., col. 978.   [3] Ibid., chap. VII, para. 17, col. 984.
[4] Ibid., para. 18, col. 985.   [5] Ibid., para. 19, col. 986.

Deum, Deus est. Verum dixi: nam et efficiens, et finalis. Ipse dat occasionem,
ipse creat affectionem, desiderium ipse consummat.'[1]

St Bernard proceeds to distinguish the four degrees through which
love must go before God is loved for himself alone. The first degree is
expounded by Traherne in the *Fourth Century*. Love is one of the four
natural affections. (The others, according to St Bernard, are fear, joy
and grief.) The very weakness of man's nature compels him to love
himself first. He must necessarily be selfish as a means of self-preserva-
tion. One can observe the truth of this in studying the behaviour of
small children, though St Bernard does not make this point. This self-
centred love, which is natural, is called by him *'amor carnalis'*.[2] This
love can become social when we find it in our own interests to love
our fellow men. Our neighbours are like ourselves and once our own
needs have been satisfied our self-love can include others: *'Sic amor*
carnalis efficitur et socialis, cum in commune protrahitur.'[3]

But if we are to love our neighbours as we ought, we must have
regard to God. We must love others in God. This is only possible if
we love God first: *'Porro in Deo diligere non potest, qui Deum non diligit.*
Oportet ergo Deum diligi prius, ut in Deo diligi possit et proximus.'[4] The
love of self must be directed to the love of God. Self-love will still
provide the basis for the higher love. Love is good; self-love, in its
proper place, is good, and therefore is a gift of God. God is already
present in love of self. He has created the possibility of love. Furthermore we owe to him our very existence, the very self which we are
jealous to protect and serve. It is in our own interest therefore to love
Him. *'Qui naturam condidit, ipse et protegit.'*[5] Furthermore we will discover in the course of the tribulations of this life that human aids will
fail, that God alone can provide enduring solace. It will come about
therefore that man, selfish by nature, loving only himself, will begin to
love God because of his own self-love. It is in his own interest to love
God because of the benefits to himself that will follow. Nothing can
be accomplished without God, and this realization will lead him to
love God as his benefactor: *'Fit itaque hoc tali modo, ut homo animalis et*
carnalis, qui praeter se neminem diligere noverat, etiam Deum vel propter se
amare incipiat, quod in ipso nimirum, ut saepe expertus est, omnia possit,
quae posse tamen prosit; et sine ipso possit nihil.'[6]

This then is the second degree of love. Man loves God not for God's
sake but still for his own sake: *'Amat ergo jam Deum sed propter se*

[1] Ibid., chap. VIII, para. 22, col. 987.   [2] Ibid., para. 23, col. 988.
[3] Ibid.   [4] Ibid., para. 25, col. 989.   [5] Ibid.   [6] Ibid.

*interim adhuc, non propter ipsum.*¹ But through the experience of the unfailing comfort and help of God in time of sufferings, even the most hardhearted of men will come to love God, not for selfish reasons, but because He is God. A crucial leap must be made. His goodness, once realized, leads us to love Him unselfishly; a new kind of love arises. We love Him in excess of our individual necessity. We have tasted and seen how gracious the Lord is. (St Bernard has Psalm 34 in mind and the theme of 'taste and see' is dominant, as we have seen, in both Traherne and John Smith.) We begin to love God as He should be loved, not for any benefits he has bestowed or will bestow, but for His own sake, because He is God. This love is its own reward, but it must not be sought simply because it is rewarding. This is the third degree or stage of love: '*Iste est tertius amoris gradus, quo jam propter se ipsum Deus diligitur.*'²

All that Traherne has written of love, and indeed much more, is contained in the *De Diligendo Deo* up to this point, and now St Bernard proceeds to speak of the fourth degree of love; of this Traherne is silent. This stage is that of the man who has ceased to love himself except in God: '*nec seipsum diligat homo nisi propter Deum*'.³ This involves the loss of the self, the absolute surrender to God: '*Te enim quodammodo perdere, tanquam qui non sis, et omnino non sentire teipsum, et a teipso exinaniri, et pene annullari, coelestis est conversationis, non humanae affectionis.*'⁴ This is not a human love but a heavenly '*conversatio*', a submission to and a communication with God. Traherne speaks on more than one occasion of conversing with God. There is a profound difference though. Traherne speaks of himself 'as God' conversing with God. He enjoys a heightened sense of his own individual possibilities in his moments of illumination; like speaks to like. Traherne is without the deep humility that St Bernard realizes. Traherne emphasizes the divine potentialities of the human person; with St Bernard it is otherwise; he knows that man is always imperfect yet can apprehend perfection. In this life we cannot achieve this fourth degree of love, this total disappearance of any love of self, of any sense of self indeed, in the love of God. We may only hope to possess it or rather be possessed by it, he writes, when we become perfect in body; in 'spiritual and immortal body'; and this cannot be achieved by any human effort: '*Itaque in corpore spirituali et immortali, in corpore integro, placido, placitoque,*

---

¹ St. Bernard, op. cit., chap. IX, para. 26, col. 989.
² Ibid., para. 26, col. 990.
³ Ibid., chap. X, para. 27, col. 990.   ⁴ Ibid.

et per omnia subjecto spiritui, speret se anima quartum apprehendere amoris gradum, vel potius in ipso apprehendi: quippe quod Dei potentiae est dare cui vult, non humanae industriae assequi.'[1]

Indeed St Bernard holds that this perfect love is to be attained only at the resurrection when souls and bodies are joined in perfect consummation. Till then the spirit will yearn for reunion with the body, for without the body it cannot be fulfilled. The body is a help to the spirit that loves God, even when it is ill, even when it is dead, and when it is raised again from the dead: *'Valet Deum diligenti animae corpus suum infirmum, valet et mortuum, valet et resuscitatum.'*[2] The flesh is a good and faithful companion to the spirit which loves the good: *'Bonus plane fidusque comes caro spiritui bono.'*[3] The body has its natural desires and appetites which demand satisfaction during life; after death we shall drink the life of the spirit and, finally, when body and soul are joined once more the consummation of the love of God is reached. It is at this point that we cease to love ourselves except for the sake of God: *'Ex hoc jam quartus ille amoris gradus perpetuo possidetur, cum summe, et solus diligitur Deus: quia nec nos ipsos jam nisi propter ipsum diligimus, ut sit ipse praemium amantium se, praemium aeternum amantium in aeternum.'*[4] This is the attainment of the fourth degree of love.

Traherne does not write of this fourth degree, but he follows St Bernard again when he writes of love as a constant and universal law. St Bernard affirms that love is the law that God Himself lives by; it is the very substance of the Godhead: *'Haec est lex aeterna, creatrix et gubernatrix universitatis.'*[5] Individuals may set up their own laws, assert an independence by making their own desires their guide, but they cannot alter the changeless order of eternal law. They may resist the law of love, but the consequence will be to endure the bondage of self: *'Hoc quippe ad aeternam justamque Dei legem pertinuit, ut qui a Deo noluit suaviter regi, poenaliter a seipso regeretur.'*[6]

It is through love that the relations between different levels of being become significant. The man who is following the law of Christian love will prefer better things to those merely good and will care for the good only because of the better. He will come to love his body not for its own sake but because of the spirit. He will love his own spirit for the sake of God and finally he will love God for Himself alone. St

---

[1] Ibid., para. 29, col. 992.
[2] Ibid., chap. XI, para. 30, col. 993.
[3] Ibid., para. 31.
[4] Ibid., para. 33, col. 995.
[5] Ibid., chap. XII, para. 33, col. 996.
[6] Ibid., chap. XIII, para. 36, col. 997.

Bernard brings his treatise to a conclusion by restating the four degrees
of love and with a confession of his own inability to achieve the perfect
condition of the fourth degree.

Traherne cannot be said to have added anything to what St Bernard
has written of love. In fact he leaves much out. What he writes does
not possess the order and clarity of St Bernard's work. Above all
Traherne changes the emphasis. He does not make the dependence of
man on God a cardinal point. He writes certainly that we must love all
things in and for God; but we are not made by Traherne to feel the
nothingness of man without God. This is characteristic of Traherne;
it is not the weakness or imperfections of humanity that form the basis
of his work. Traherne sees man as in harmony with his world fundamentally; he is possessed of unlimited powers for good. St Bernard's
vision is more profound, indeed, more Christian. He begins from the
facts of our animal nature and on that base constructs his careful
discipline. At every point we are aware of but never depressed by the
limited nature of the individual, and we are taken as far as the individual
by himself can go. The great difference between the two is that whereas
St Bernard holds that though man can approach perfection and perform
acts which partake of perfection he can not himself be perfect, Traherne
holds that man can put himself 'in frame' and become God-like, think
divine thoughts. Traherne has less sense of objective values, that is. He
is at a point where the religious attitude and the humanist attitude are
confused. What to St Bernard are absolute objective realities are becoming for Traherne uncertain in their location; we have noted already
that the problem of evil for him seems no more than a lack of harmony,
a disproportion in relations. We find in Traherne an increase in subjectivity in regard to values; the divine is being ascribed to the human.
The perfection that properly belongs to the non-human is, in Traherne's
thought, projected into human experiences and relations.

I say 'being' quite deliberately. Traherne does not hold a clearly
defined position. He is a man passing from one stage to another. He
shows a mixture, a confusion of attitudes. It is not clarity or order that
is characteristic of him but wonder, which, as T. E. Hulme points out,
can never be a permanently fixed thing. I have claimed elsewhere that
Traherne's vision is theocentric; but this vision is not constant or steady.
In his most distinctive utterances Traherne apprehends the human and
the divine as approaching a level of equivalence. Moreover he seems
unaware of the implications of such an approximation. A study of the
De Diligendo Deo can leave us in no doubt on this issue. The greater

work throws into relief the limitations of the lesser without detriment to any of its real virtues. Because of the *De Diligendo Deo* the *Centuries* can be read with a more enduring effect than otherwise they could achieve.

CHAPTER IX

Traherne and a Romantic Heresy

THE work of T. E. Hulme, whether one agrees with him or not, is still relevant for any discussion today which is concerned with attitudes or conceptions which may be called religious, and his essay 'Romanticism and classicism'[1] is so close in certain ways to Traherne's thinking that it will serve as a further point of contact between Traherne and the modern world.

Hulme considers these two terms as indicative not simply of literary fashions or preference, or as referring only to particular historical periods. They may do so, of course, but they indicate also general attitudes to life, attitudes which result from our religious convictions:

> Here is the root of all romanticism: that man, the individual, is an infinite reservoir of possibilities; and if you can so rearrange society by the destruction of oppressive order then these possibilities will have a chance and you will get Progress.
>
> One can define the classical quite clearly as the exact opposite to this. Man is an extraordinarily fixed and limited animal whose nature is absolutely constant. It is only by tradition and organisation that anything decent can be got out of him. . . .
>
> Put shortly, these are the two views, then. One, that man is intrinsically good, spoilt by circumstance; and the other that he is intrinsically limited, but disciplined by order and tradition to something fairly decent. To the one party man's nature is like a well, to the other like a bucket. The view which regards man as a well, a reservoir full of possibilities, I call the romantic; the one which regards him as a very finite and fixed creature, I call the classical.
>
> One may note here that the Church has always taken the classical view since the defeat of the Pelagian heresy and the adoption of the sane classical dogma of original sin.[2]

The difference, then, between the romantic and the classical is not simply that between exuberance and restraint, or between 'subjects' and forms of writing; it involves two very different conceptions of human nature and of the problem of good and evil. For instance, it is

[1] T. E. Hulme, *Speculations* (London, 1924), p. 113.
[2] Op. cit., pp. 116–17.

possible to say, according to this definition, that a 'classical' writer is committed to the view that human nature must acknowledge its limitations, must realize what it is not, in traditional language, must constantly avow the need for humility, the most difficult of virtues.

Hulme clearly intends his definition to be used outside the limits of the so-called Romantic period. He uses it of Shakespeare whom he describes as 'the classic of motion' and of Racine who presents a classicism which is static. On the face of it, Traherne would seem to fit completely into Hulme's definition of the romantic attitude. For Traherne, human nature is an infinite reservoir of possibilities: 'the soul is a miraculous abyss of infinite abysses, an undrainable ocean, an unexhausted fountain of endless oceans' (*Centuries*, II, 83). Its essence is capacity. We may all enjoy a paradise on earth if we get rid of the evil effects of custom and education. We are all potentially god-like: 'Here is love! Here is a Kingdom! Where all are knit in infinite unity. All are happy in each other. All are like Deities. Every one the end of all things, every one supreme, everyone a treasure and the joy of all, and everyone most infinitely delighted in being so' (*Centuries*, I, 74). This and similar passages are the enthusiastic utterance of one whose eyes have been dazzled by the vision of man as the image of God. But man is not God though he may contain within him a divine spark. Here is the link with Hulme's definition. The implication is that since romanticism is the 'exact opposite' of classicism and classicism has been the attitude of the Church 'since the defeat of the Pelagian heresy', then romanticism, in Hulme's sense, and the Pelagian heresy are in some way associated.

Whether or not we choose to call Traherne a romantic, in Hulme's sense, it must be admitted that elements of the Pelagian heresy are present in his thought. There is relevance in bringing in this old controversy (Pelagius' dates are A.D. c. 360–c. 420) because although rejected, as Hulme says, by orthodox teaching, the Pelagian theory appears in one form or another in many of our contemporary panaceas in social and political life, which promise salvation in a variety of terms by alleviating man's external circumstances. This done, one is required to assume, man's natural goodness will be free to express itself in a world which will then be perfect.

Pelagius was not so much the originator as the exponent of a theory of holiness.[1] This theory questions the need of divine grace for man to

[1] B. J. Kidd, in *A History of the Church to A.D. 461* (Oxford, 1922), vol. III, gives a detailed account of Pelagianism.

achieve good. He may do so unaided, through his own deliberate choice. This is possible since God has given man free will as part of the endowment of our nature, and this power is still effective. We can, if we choose, be without sin even if sin be taken to include imperfections within the spirit. Such a view is the very antithesis of the thought and feeling of Donne in his *Holy Sonnets* for instance. But Traherne's most characteristic thought is in line with much of this. Pelagius held that there is no original sin and that there was no Fall with all its inevitable consequences for the posterity of Adam and Eve. In infancy we are all in the position of our first parents, free to become either good or evil. 'Sin is a personal and voluntary thing and only begins where responsibility begins. There is no need of grace. All we have to do is to exert our will, and to use the nature that God gave us.'[1]

The main points of the Pelagian view are as follows. Man is a free agent. There exists unconditional freedom of the will, and this freedom consists in 'the possibility of yielding to, or abstaining from, sin, at pleasure'.[2] An individual can abstain from doing good or willing to do good but he possesses the power both to do and to will it. The power 'belongs properly to God, who gave it me when He made me; but the other two—to desire and to be—rest with me, because they have their source in my will. And praise is due to me in proportion to my good will and good deeds.'[3] Traherne's thought is similar. '... We may sin or we may be holy' (*Centuries*, II, 97).

> God made man a free agent for his own advantage, and left him in the hand of his own counsel, that he might be the more glorious.—For He thereby committed to their [i.e. His creatures] hands a power to do that which He infinitely hated, which nothing certainly could move Him to entrust them with, but some infinite benefit which might be attained thereby, what that was, if you desire to know, it was the excellency, dignity and exaltation of His creature (*Centuries*, IV, 42).

The parallel is close. Man having power to do good or to sin ('to do that which He infinitely hated') is all the more to be praised if he chooses to do good.

A second point is the assertion that it is possible to live without sin. The Pelagian holds that there is nothing to prevent a man living an absolutely sinless existence. It follows that if sin is voluntary then 'there is no such thing as Original Sin, i.e. a propensity to sin which we each

---

[1] Kidd, op. cit., p. 55.
[2] Pelagius, *Libellus Fidei*, para. 13.
[3] Pelagius, *Pro libero arbitrio*, *ap*. Aug. *De gratia Christi*, para. 5.

inherit through our *origo* or birth'.[1] Further, our present nature is not impaired by any Fall.[2] Nature is as sufficient now, as ever it was. We can all be as Adam was if we so wish. Sin comes through habit; it becomes second nature through evil influences.

Traherne endeavours to maintain his orthodoxy: 'Yet is all our corruption derived from Adam: inasmuch as all the evil examples and inclinations of the world arise from his sin' (*Centuries*, III, 8). But his own experiences of childhood splendour incline him to the Pelagian view: 'our misery proceedeth ten thousand times more from the outward bondage of opinion and custom, than from any inward corruption or depravation of Nature: And that it is not our parents' loins, so much as our parents' lives, that enthrals and blinds us' (*Centuries*, III, 8). Nature is itself good and nature includes 'our Souls and Bodies, with all their faculties, senses and endowments' (*Centuries*, III, 9). Sin comes in through art and error, through artificiality, through sophistication. Traherne comes close to the Pelagian assertion that we can live the sinless life as Adam did: 'I am sure those barbarous people that go naked, come nearer to Adam, God, and Angels in the simplicity of their wealth, though not in Knowledge' (*Centuries*, III, 12).

The intense experience of the beauty of Nature and the full assurance that this beauty is a revelation of Divine goodness is for Traherne the great solvent of the bondage of evil: 'No man can sin that clearly seeth the beauty of God's face: because no man can sin against his own happiness, that is, none can when he sees it clearly, willingly, and wittingly forsake it, tempter, temptation, loss and danger being all seen' (*Centuries*, II, 97). This passage expresses again the voluntary and personal nature of this conception of sin. Sin lies in the failure to see the divine pattern in the world. Once this is realized sin becomes impossible. An orthodox criticism of this would be that redemption by Christ's sacrifice, the death of God, becomes thereby meaningless, a pointless execution. The individual can save himself unaided through the virtue of what is, as Traherne has phrased it, an aesthetic experience. Traherne has no sense of the terrible spiritual torment that the conviction of sin as an objective fact in the nature of things can cause. The solution seems easy for him. All that we should do is to bring a heart that watches and receives to achieve the holiness and righteousness which 'naturally flow out of our fruition of the World: for who can vilify and

[1] Kidd, op. cit., p. 60.
[2] For an explicit denial by Pelagius of Original Sin, see his words quoted in Aug. *De pecc. orig.*, para. 14.

debase himself by any sin, while he actually considers he is the heir of it? It exalts a man to a sublime and honorable life: it lifts him above lusts and makes him angelical' (*Centuries*, II, 97). We see again how Traherne is not concerned with any sense of the limitations of human nature but rather with its great powers and endowments. It is 'the infinite extent of the understanding and affection of the soul' (*Centuries*, IV, 100) which can indeed comprehend God and 'the universal beauty of God's Kingdom' (*Centuries*, IV, 99) upon which Traherne bases his confidence. We read nothing in him of the necessity for grace. We have argued that Traherne holds this view because he sees man, the natural man, as the image of God. The dangers of such a view remain neverthe-less.[1] What is there to prevent a man from asserting his own holiness in his own right? and from this point moving to the deification and the idolatry of the human individual with all the consequences with which our present times are only too closely familiar?

It is not strange to find in Traherne traces of heresy. The years in which he lived were marked by diversity and independence of belief, by the multiplicity of sectarian doctrines[2] as well as by the growth of the idea of religious toleration. For instance a great many Independent theorists held that no 'power over conscience has been given by God to any man or any earthly authority. . . . The ultimate authority in finding and interpreting God's truth is the individual Christian who possesses all the guidance which a synod or a Parliament enjoys for determining between truth and error.'[3] This itself, of course, could be regarded as an heretical belief. The problem is to determine the limits to which toleration should go. In modern times Hulme had no doubt that the 'sane classical dogma of original sin' should be maintained in the Anglican church; whereas Traherne would hardly have been accused of unorthodoxy by many of his contemporaries.

Furthermore Traherne was not a systematic or consistent writer. The *Centuries* contain a series of meditations on the cross especially in the second half of the *First Century*. There is, however, no resolution of the contradiction which seems to exist between these meditations and his characteristic dilution of a sense of the necessity for redemption. What remains as remarkable in Traherne is not so much the quality of his

[1] 'Pelagius by denying Original Sin, argued against the necessity for redemption, and struck at the root of Christianity.' J. Michelet, *History of France*, I, p. 30.

[2] See Whiting, *Studies in English Puritanism, 1660–1688* (London, 1931).

[3] W. K. Jordan, *The Development of Religious Toleration in England, 1640–1660* (London, 1938), p. 438.

theological thinking or the nature of his orthodoxy as his splendid expression of a vivid sense of being one with the universe and yet at the same time an individual, unique, 'the sole heir'. It is this which is to be valued in Traherne and which is his contribution to our knowledge of one of the kinds of supreme happiness possible to men: 'You never enjoy the world aright, till the Sea itself floweth in your veins, till you are clothed with the heavens and crowned with the stars: and perceive yourself to be the sole heir of the whole world, and more than so, because men are in it who are every one sole heirs as well as you. Till you can sing and rejoice and delight in God, as misers do in gold, and Kings in sceptres, you never enjoy the world.'

The Discovery of the 'Poems' and 'Centuries'

THE story of the finding of the manuscripts of the *Poems* and *Centuries* and the final ascription of their authorship to Traherne is one of the most exciting accounts of good fortune, well used, and of skilful literary detective work in the history of English literature.

The manuscripts were first acquired by Mr W. T. Brooke in London during the winter of 1896–7 when he bought two well-preserved volumes, very cheaply, from a second-hand bookstall in the Farringdon Road. One was a folio, the other a small octavo. The first half of the folio contained poetry, the second, prose extracts and notes, arranged in alphabetical order beginning with 'Aristotles Philosophie' and ending with 'Virtue'. The octavo contained short prose passages with a few poems interspersed. These were the *Centuries*. There was no indication at all of who the author was.

Brooke was inclined to think that the poems were by Henry Vaughan and he showed his manuscripts to the editor Alexander Grosart, who agreed in this view of their authorship. Grosart then bought the two manuscripts from Brooke, intending to incorporate the newly found poems in his projected edition of Vaughan. In fact, he added the lettering 'MSS. of Henry Vaughan Silurist', to the volumes that Brooke had originally found. However, Grosart died in 1899 before producing this new edition.

The news of the discovery of these manuscripts, whether or not the work of Henry Vaughan, had naturally spread in literary and scholarly circles. Bertram Dobell, a bookseller, and editor of the poems of James Thomson, was sufficiently interested from Brooke's account to make a study of the manuscripts which were now in the possession of Charles Higham, another well-known bookseller, who had bought Grosart's library. Dobell was a friend of Higham and was thus able to buy both the folio and octavo volumes from him.

Dobell was more than simply an enterprising bookseller; he was clearly a man of remarkable literary perceptiveness and he became convinced that the poems now in his possession, though showing resemblances in form and in subject matter, were, in fact, not the work of Vaughan at all. Brooke now appears again in a minor but crucial rôle. He had read in the British Museum an anonymous work, *A Serious and Patheticall Contemplation of the Mercies of God*, which contained a number of poems in free verse called *Thanksgivings*. He copied out for Dobell, who was keen to find the author of his manuscripts, the rhymed pieces in the *Contemplation*. Dobell's sense of literature was right again. Just as he felt that Vaughan was not the author so he felt sure that the man who had written the *Thanksgivings* was also the man who had written the poetry and prose in his two books. The Address 'To the Reader' of the *Thanksgivings* stated that the author had been 'to the service of the late Lord Keeper Bridgeman as his Chaplain'. Anthony à Wood's *Athenae Oxonienses* served to identify this chaplain as Thomas Traherne, author of *Roman Forgeries* and *Christian Ethics*. The final certainty came with Dobell's finding in the prose of *Christian Ethics* a verse excerpt beginning 'As in a Clock' which was identical, with some variations, with a passage in one of his manuscripts, in *Centuries*, III, 21.

Dobell brought out the first edition to be printed of Traherne's poems in 1903; the *Centuries* followed in 1908. In the introduction to the editions of 1903, 1906 and 1932 a full account is given of the stages in which this piece of literary detection was triumphantly concluded.

Published and Unpublished Writings

THE known writings of Thomas Traherne, in order of publication, are as follows:

1. *Roman Forgeries*, by A Faithful Son of the Church of England (1673).
2. *Daily Devotions, consisting of Thanksgivings, Confessions and Prayers*, by a Humble Penitent (1673).
3. *Christian Ethicks* (1675).
4. *The Soul's Communion with Her Saviour*. The original, 'reduced' by Philip Traherne, and published by him with that title (1685).
5. *A Serious and Patheticall Contemplation of the Mercies of God, in several most Devout and Sublime Thanksgivings for the Same*. Published 'by the Reverend Doctor Hickes at the request of a friend of the Author's' (1699).
6. *Hexameron or Meditations on the Six Days of Creation, and Meditations and Devotions on the Life of Christ*. Published by Nathaniel Spinckes as Parts I and II of *A Collection of Meditations and Devotions* in three Parts. Part II, *Meditations and Devotions on the Life of Christ*, is the original, unreduced, of No. 4 above. Part III of the collection is a reprint of No. 2 above (1717).
7. *Poems of Thomas Traherne*. Published by Bertram Dobell. Contains the poems in the Dobell Folio MS. (1903).
8. *Centuries of Meditations*. Published by Dobell, from the untitled octavo Dobell MS. (1908).
9. *Poems of Felicity*. Published by Dr Bell, from the British Museum MS. Burney 392, which is Philip Traherne's copy of a now lost original (1910).
10. *The Poetical Works of Thomas Traherne*. Edited by Gladys I. Wade, and published by P. J. and A. E. Dobell. Contains the poems of Traherne from all sources (1932).
11. Thomas Traherne, *Centuries, Poems and Thanksgivings*, ed. H. M. Margoliouth, two volumes (1958).

In addition to these published writings, there are some works of Traherne still in manuscript. They include:

1. *The Book of Private Devotions*. An octavo Dobell MS.
2. A small collection of early verse. Also a Dobell MS.
3. *A Commonplace Book*, the second half of the Dobell Folio.
4. A student's notebook. British Museum Burney MS. 126.

Index